Table of Contents

In the Beginning . . . Dads

What Fatherhood Was Supposed to Be, and What Happened to It
(Genesis 1–3)

By

Tony Papadakis

Bible quotes taken from New American Standard Bible®, Copyright © 1960, 1971, 1977, 1995 by The Lockman Foundation. All rights reserved.

Publisher: Anegnote Press
Mechanicsville, MD

This book is dedicated to my late wife Lori.
You were simply the best, and it ended too soon.

Introduction

S TOP! Read this first!

This book is not intended to take you to the finish line of fatherhood. This is only the starting line. It is the beginning of the journey of fatherhood, not the end of it. This is the first in the Fatherhood in Genesis series, a collection of books looking at what Genesis can teach us about fatherhood. It may surprise you to learn that fatherhood is one of the central topics of the book of Genesis. In fact, the Bible teaches about fatherhood alongside many of the most crucial passages of the Bible's main message of salvation. Accordingly, future books will cover fatherhood in the Law of Moses (Exodus through Deuteronomy), fatherhood in the history of Israel (Judges through Esther), fatherhood in biblical wisdom literature (Job through Ecclesiastes), fatherhood in the biblical prophets (Isaiah through Malachi), and fatherhood in the New Testament. Throughout the Bible, the topic of fatherhood runs parallel to the Bible's main teachings. It is simply impossible to cover it all in a single book. So, rather than rush through it, the Fatherhood in Genesis series will take its time, allowing the reader to consider all the lessons on fatherhood included in Genesis.

To paraphrase an often used saying, fatherhood is not a sprint—it's a marathon. One of the main purposes of this book is to train you for the long haul of fatherhood. There are no quick tips, easy-to-use suggestions, or gimmicky life hacks here. Fatherhood is too important to be trivialized like that. Instead, this book will allow you to listen in on a series of conversations between two men talking about fatherhood in Genesis. The conversations are focused but unhurried.

Why is this topic presented as a conversation? Because I believe that we learn best when we just talk to other people. However, since I cannot personally talk to each reader, I wanted to write this as if it were a conversation. Personally, I am drawn to conversations. I prefer listening to podcasts that are conversations between two people. And I am drawn to the parables of Jesus that are stories of conversations. Finally, I have been impressed by Ken Blanchard's books that were little more than conversations. In fact, readers who are familiar with Blanchard's books may be tempted to think I am imitating him in this book. That thought is not wrong.

The bottom line is that I love stories. It doesn't matter how the story is told; I love stories. I'll read a story, I'll listen to a story, and I'll watch a story. The more stories I get, the more I want.

God hardwired humans for stories. Stories speak to us at a much deeper level than anything else except perhaps music. Music, however, lacks the breadth of stories. Music can handle a small subject, but stories can handle big subjects with both depth and breadth. We continue to talk about stories long after we've stopped talking about an individual song.

My favorite passages of Scripture are the stories. The brilliance of the parables is that they are stories within stories, or a story from Jesus told as told by someone telling the story of Jesus's life and ministry. The more I read those parables, the more alive they become. I may grow tired of songs, but I never grow tired of a well-told story.

That is why I have written this book as a story. Stories communicate and teach at a deeper level than writing that is simply informational—like this introduction—can do. Writing that reflects the reality we all live in touches us in ways that other writing simply cannot. This book is nothing more than a story. It is the story of one man, Peter, mentoring a young father, Brian, in the ways of fatherhood. He does so using the first nine chapters of Genesis.

Why This Book?

I spent sixteen years as a nonresident father. My ex and I split up when our youngest of three was two years old (our oldest was five). Six years later, I married Lori who had a son, Vincent, from her previous marriage. During my time as a father, I was a residential father, a nonresidential father, a stepfather, and a residential father again when two of my three came to live with me for a couple of years. The only thing I haven't done is adopted fatherhood.

Twelve years ago, in 2010, I completed my master's thesis for seminary. My topic was a theology of fatherhood for nonresident fathers. When I went looking for sources, I was shocked at how little information there was on this topic. There were many self-help books for fathers, but they focused on residential fathers, men who lived with their children. For a nonresidential father, the few books available were of little benefit. Although there were some non-Christian books focused on nonresidential fathers, they emphasized things like the importance of being on time for pickup and drop-off, making sure child support is paid, and playing nice with the children's mother. My responses to these unhelpful suggestions were (1) The parent who has to get the kiddos together is *always* late for pickup and drop-off, and there's a fantastic reason for that—kids don't give a fig about schedules!; (2) Child support is now monitored through a state government agency (the Department for Child Support Enforcement [DCSE] in Virginia). These guys make the mafia seem like a warm, cuddly teddy bear by comparison. As the nonresidential father, I could call DCSE and enjoy the privilege of being treated like some sort of child rapist, someone who was beneath contempt. With DCSE, I was always guilty until proven somewhat slightly less guilty. I could appreciate that the people who work there have a crummy job, but . . . *wow*! Worst of all, I was the one who asked DCSE to get involved because my ex was making claims about child support which were wrong. I needed a neutral third party to keep the records. Finally, (3) if I had been able to "play nice" with my ex, then for the sake of my kiddos I would still be married to her—*duh!* In short, I found these books, even the ones that claimed to "talk tough," to be so much fluff and nonsense.

I was able to find a plethora of books devoted to single moms. Books for nonresidential fathers, however, were few, and none were all that helpful.

On the web, I found numerous sites devoted to nonresidential fathers. These, however, fell into two categories. The first category was defunct. A nonresidential father wanted to set up a platform but then got distracted by the busyness of life. The second category was the "fuss" board. These sites degenerated into men griping about their exes in terms of money, visitation, medical bills, and legal issues. Again, these did not help me understand fatherhood so much as the practical realities of being a nonresidential father . . . as if I didn't already know about those things!

Finally, my church experience was equally unhelpful. Churches are set up for full-time parents who want to drop off their kids so they can have some adult time. Often people encouraged me to come to a church event on a visitation weekend. They thought telling me that childcare was available would entice me to come. I always declined those invitations. I did not want to drop off my children; I wanted help learning how to interact with these children who were increasingly becoming total strangers to me. And, frankly, I have seen a lot of full-time parents who could have used the same help with their children. I can't help but think that church youth programs have it backward. Rather than provide a means of dropping off their children for someone else to take care of, I wonder what would happen if they had programs that helped parents and their children engage in positive, healthy interactions. How might such programs strengthen families rather than separating parents from their children for an hour or so? A simple family game night at church might be worth more than a year of Bible studies.

So, what did I find in my search for help? No books. No blogs. No help from church. How, then, was I supposed to write this thesis?

Where was I supposed to turn for help? I wrote my thesis in three parts. The first part was looking at psychology research in the field of divorce and fatherhood. That was sobering stuff! However, I footnoted it correctly because there was plenty of material. But the next two sections got increasingly thin on references simply because there were none. In my thesis is a footnote about two-thirds of the way in that addresses the issue. I claimed that the paper was a "seed theology" and that no references exist. I was attempting to deal with the fact that no sources covered the topics.

Since 2010 when I completed my thesis, Christians have published more books aimed at nonresidential fathers. However, they are mostly pastoral in nature. By that I mean a concerned pastor wrote a book based more on his pastoral care of nonresidential fathers in his congregation than a systematic exploration of Scripture. They are not theological works that provide a road map for understanding fatherhood; they are books to help men navigate the situation they are in. They are more about surviving, less about thriving, and certainly not about describing truly biblical fatherhood. If these books can be used of God, then fantastic. However, the reality is that there is still limited work done on a true biblical theology of fatherhood.

As a Christian, I made three decisions that shaped how I approached being a nonresident father, and they all found their way into my thesis. First, I made a commitment that I would not be a "Disney Dad." I mean that a weekend with Dad was not going to be a trip to a theme park or concert or some big event. They were too expensive (I couldn't afford them), I'm not a big fan of them in the first place (I would have been miserable), and most importantly, they prevented me from interacting with my kiddos. Roller coasters may be fun, but a theme park is not a great place to get to know your children.

Second, as a Christian, I wanted to know what the Bible said about fatherhood. Although I could find nothing in the popular Christian press,[1] I saw the issue of fatherhood lurking just underneath numerous biblical stories. I wanted to mine those stories for what they taught. I did not want to "proof text" my view of fatherhood, that is, find verses that seem to support my American view of fatherhood and claim that this is what the Bible teaches. However, it was not until I entered my PhD program in Biblical Studies that I had the opportunity to fully examine these stories. When I did my first two searches for scholarly research on what the Bible teaches about fatherhood, I found some sociological material about family life in the ancient Near East. However, these were not theologies of fatherhood so much as descriptions of the views and practices of fatherhood that found their way into Scripture. As a Christian, I believe that the Scriptures are God-breathed. I am more interested in God's view of fatherhood than I am about which sociological tendencies God used to declare His truth. On my third pass, I found a little work done by Roman Catholic scholars, but not much. I was (and continue to be) stunned that such an obviously important topic has been totally neglected for two thousand years. This book is the first step of a journey to rectify this glaring oversight.

The third decision I made was that I would learn to play with my children. And by play, I mean use our imaginations and play the way I did as a kid. I didn't grow up with video games and online videos on demand. We just made it up. "Hey, I found a box—let's have fun!" Every Saturday, my neighborhood became a scene from *Lord of the Flies* until the sun went down. When the streetlights came on, it was time to go home. Although I didn't want my kids running around *Lord of the Flies* style, I did want them to learn how to play with their imaginations. To that end, I had a pirate weekend, a spy weekend, and several weekends featuring a murder mystery (*Who Killed Santa's Chef?* was an instant classic!) and treasure hunts. I learned the value of old-fashioned board games to generate unstructured time with the kiddos. *Clue* was a constant favorite, and I learned some surprising things about my kiddos playing *Life*. Play is the language of children, and I determined to be fluent in it. Even as my children became teens and young adults, those times we spent in play are magical memories.

And when I can get Steam to work correctly on my computer, I still hop online and play *Age of Empires* or *World of Warships* with my now adult son. I should note that the laser tag story Peter tells is a true story. My late wife Lori found a laser tag set that worked in broad daylight. Lori's son, Vincent, had the drop on me, and then Lori tagged me out. I clearly remember the self-satisfied smirk on her face when we were done with that round. It's one of my most cherished memories of those days.

This series is meant to be something in between a pastoral book and an academic theological work. A systematic understanding of what the Bible says about fatherhood is critical to comprehending how we as fathers should act, no matter if we are residential fathers or nonresidential. There is an old saying that I think is true: "For as he thinks within himself, so he is" (Proverbs 23:7). If we don't help fathers think biblically about fatherhood, we cannot expect them to act like biblical fathers.

My heart is with nonresidential fathers. I strongly believe that any understanding of fatherhood that does not address nonresidential fatherhood is seriously deficient. Today, only one-third of children in America will reach eighteen while still living with both their biological parents. Just 33 percent. That statistic is staggering. But to my mind, the immediate implication is that our understanding of fatherhood must address nonresidential fatherhood if it is to be useful to most men. That is why this book presents two men who learn fatherhood through the lens of their experience as nonresidential fathers. I do not present them as living out an ideal situation that is better than residential fathers. Nor do I make any comment on divorce or the structure of families. Instead, I present these two men as representative of a difficult situation that many men face. If we can understand biblical fatherhood for their situation, I am firmly convinced that we can understand it for all fathers.

What About Mothers?

The primary focus of this book is on fatherhood, not motherhood, as found in Genesis 1–3. Motherhood is almost a passing subject, and most of that is found in the Epilogue. This is not meant as a slight or to demean women. I am simply following the text of Genesis, and the role of mothers is first discussed in Genesis 4. Prior to that, the best we have is that Eve was created to be Adam's helper and that she was created to be equal in dignity and standing (Gen 1:26–27; 2:22). However, Genesis 2 and 3 focus on the roles and responsibilities of Adam, not Eve. Although we can infer that both shared in the same roles, we will see that they do not participate equally in those roles. I leave a fuller discussion of this to the Epilogue.

How to Use This Book

This book is intended to be used in one of three ways.

First, it can be read by an individual for personal enrichment. My desire is for fathers to develop a biblical understanding of fatherhood and, more importantly, to live it out with their children. My prayer is that this book helps to get you there. If it doesn't, I pray you find someone or something that does.

Second, it can be read within the context of a mentoring relationship, like the relationship between Peter and Brian depicted in this book. This may be informal mentoring or perhaps pastoral counseling. In these cases, the mentor should decide how much or how little of the book to use depending on where the mentee is in his personal circumstances. One-on-one mentoring is a lost art in America, and such mentoring is the backbone of father–child relationships. It is not just the children who are built up through one-on-one mentoring; the father is too. When the mentor models fatherhood in these relationships, he prepares the "child" to become a "father" to someone else.

Finally, this book can be read as part of a men's ministry. Group leaders can decide how much or how little of the book to use depending on the needs of the group. However, there should be plenty of material to talk about in the stories themselves. The provided questions have been written to elicit a rich discussion.

Personal Guide

This book has a corresponding personal guide that can be downloaded for free at tonypapadakis.com/downloads. I strongly encourage you to download and use it as you read through this book. The personal guide will provide the tools you need to implement the steps that Peter lays out for Brian. It will walk you through implementing a plan for fatherhood and living it out in a loving yet deliberate manner. This is the same plan I used with my children. I have been blessed by it, and I know you will be too.

God bless you in your journey toward biblical fatherhood.

Tony Papadakis
Mechanicsville, MD
October 2022

1 Drop-Off

Fifteen minutes late . . . again!

Brian had texted Bethany before leaving to let her know he was running late. He was trying to be courteous, but it wouldn't matter. All she cared about was that he was not there on time, so she had to wait. He knew she would be fuming in the car. There was no sense trying to tell her that Megan couldn't find her favorite stuffed animal, a gray dolphin she called Tuna. Nor should he bother explaining that Brian Jr. had pried off the air vent on the floor and stuffed all his clothing in it, which he had only discovered when Brian Jr. said he couldn't find his clothes to pack. None of it made any difference. Brian was late for drop-off again (after a weekend visit) and that's all Bethany would focus on.

Brian knew that if he attempted to explain why he was late, Bethany would dismiss whatever he said. She would say, "I have them every day, and yet I manage to be on time!" Of course, she was rarely on time, but he knew from experience that the facts would only make the situation worse. Any explanation meant to elicit sympathy was a lost cause with Bethany.

Brian turned into the parking lot of the fast-food restaurant that was roughly halfway between his and Bethany's homes. As he slowed the car and the front tires made the familiar *bump-bump* into the parking lot, Megan and Brian Jr. looked up from their video games and saw their mother's minivan. "It's Mom!" In that instant, the entire air in the car changed. The kids went from disinterested disengagement to ecstatic excitement at seeing their mother. At pickup on Friday, the kids had to be coaxed into his car. Now on Sunday afternoon they were thrilled to be getting back to Mom and their normal life. It made Brian's heart ache—that constant reminder that his own kids did not enjoy their time with him. It was the final stab in his heart of a mediocre weekend with their dad. He wasn't a bad father, but he wasn't a good one either. And he knew it. And his ex knew it. And, worst of all, his own children knew it.

He parked, stepped out, and apologized again for being late over the roof of his car. Bethany didn't reply. Instead, she smiled at Megan, opened the back door closest to her, and unbuckled her daughter. Brian unbuckled his son. The kids quickly grabbed their bags, threw them into Mom's minivan, and clambered into their seats.

This was the moment Brian dreaded the most. He could handle the cutting remarks from his ex. He could rationalize being broke all the time. But it was this moment that happened every drop-off that was a dagger to his heart. It wasn't seeing the kiddos drive off. No, he had gotten used to that a long time ago. It was Bethany coaxing the children out of the minivan to say goodbye to their father. They had been in such a hurry to leave and get back to their normal lives that they forgot their dad as soon as they saw their mom.

"Don't you want to say goodbye to your dad?" Bethany said with a fake smile and insincere enthusiasm. The kids hesitated. Clearly, they just wanted to leave. But obediently, they climbed out of the minivan for the perfunctory Sunday afternoon hug. Brian wanted to gather them in his arms and tell them how much he loved them. However, they gave quick hugs, and, as usual, words failed him. Words always seemed to fail him when talking to his children. They jumped quickly back into the minivan. Bethany buckled in Brian Jr., and Brian buckled in Megan. He gently brushed aside her uncombed hair (he had run out of time to comb it before heading out), kissed her forehead, and said goodbye.

Bethany, already in the driver's seat, pushed the button to close the two sliding doors. Brian waved and said another goodbye, but they were too busy talking excitedly with their mother to notice. They never talked to him like that.

Bethany backed the minivan out and left.

Another weekend with his kids. Another weekend to remind him that his children were growing up without him. Another weekend to mark the widening relational chasm between him and his children. Brian had no idea how to bridge that chasm. *I'm not a father*, he thought bitterly; he was an every-other-weekend babysitter. It was the end of another weekend that began with the hope of reconnecting with his children, and yet finished with another thud. Another weekend to remind him that his own children had become near strangers to him. Another wasted weekend with his children. Part of him wondered why he even bothered to keep doing this. Why not just admit defeat and bail out? But that was a question he would not seriously entertain. He reminded himself that he would do the right thing even if he failed . But rather than give him resolve, it was like punching himself in the gut. He knew he was failing, and he was failing spectacularly. He exhaled and his shoulders sank further.

"Tough weekend with your kids?" asked someone standing next to him.

"Yeah, it sure was," Brian replied without thinking. Then suddenly he was shaken from his thoughts. *Wait a minute, who is this?* he asked himself.

Turning to see who had just spoken to him, Brian wasn't sure what to make of this man. He was of average height and average build. He wore nondescript clothing, but he was clearly a yuppie of some sort, perhaps an academic yuppie. His hair looked like someone put a large bowl on his head and cut off whatever stuck out from the rim. Mostly dark with streaks of gray, the hair started from the top of his head and stuck straight down in every direction with a cut-out for his glasses. His glasses were slightly too large for his face. Behind the glasses were a pair of eyes that betrayed intelligence and wisdom. Yet his smile grabbed Brian's attention. It was a crooked smile pulled slightly to one side, as if he were laughing at some inner joke of extreme irony. It was the quizzical smile of a man who knew deep sorrow, but his joy outweighed his sorrow. It was a joy that was completely out of place in Brian's moment of personal despair. It was a joy that was a million miles away from Brian.

"Hi, I'm Peter Lee, but my friends call me P. Lee," he said, holding out his hand.

Who the heck is this guy? Brian asked himself. Yet, he seemed okay. After a moment's hesitation, he shook Peter's hand tentatively. "I'm Brian."

"I'm sorry to intrude, but I was getting out of my car when I saw you dropping off your children. It reminded me of all the years I did the same thing with my kiddos." He looked away for a moment, his smile fading a little as he remembered. "Yeah, picking them up every other Friday and dropping them off Sunday afternoon. Those were good days . . . very good days . . . and tough days." Brian watched Peter get lost in his own thoughts. He wondered how this man had done with his own kids. *Better than me, certainly. I can't imagine someone being much worse than me.*

After a moment, Peter stopped reminiscing and focused on Brian again, his quizzical smile back on his face. "It's tough getting the kids back on time, isn't it?"

Brian's first thought was to leave, yet there was something about this man that made him stay. He sensed that this was a good man. "Yeah, it is. It's tougher when one of the kids stuffs all his clothes into the air-conditioning vent."

Peter threw his head back in genuine laughter. It was the laughter of a man who could say, "Been there, done that!" but was really, "Been there, done that, and I really miss it." Now that Bethany had left, Brian could see the humor of it, too, and joined Peter in laughter.

Peter said, "Once, when I had my kiddos over, my son discovered my paper shredder. I had it next to my filing cabinet. He thought it was the coolest toy ever. So, after he shredded all my bills for that month—"

"Seriously?" Brian blurted out.

"Yeah. I went to paperless bills after that." They both laughed. "Anyway, after shredding all my bills, he opened a drawer and started shredding my mortgage documents."

"No!"

"Oh, yeah," Peter said, still laughing. "He was about halfway through before I caught him."

"What did you do?"

"Well, I seriously considered dropping him off the roof. But then I decided that the police and my ex would take a dim view of that. I moved the shredder out of his reach, and later I installed a lock on the door to my office. I can laugh about it now, but at the time I was furious."

"I can see why."

"Yeah. Well, hey, they're only documents, and documents can be replaced. But that moment is now a precious memory for me, and memories can't be replaced." Peter paused. "Listen, I know you don't know me; I'm just a stranger in a parking lot. But I can tell you're struggling to make this every-other-weekend thing work with your kiddos." He held up his hand to stop Brian from protesting. "I know the look. I've been there. I had to struggle through the exact same things you're going through now. Tell you what; come inside with me, I'll buy you dinner, and let's talk. Let me share with you some of what I learned. What have you got to lose? A few minutes of your time? C'mon." Then Peter turned and walked to the front door of the restaurant.

Brian hesitated. *Who is this guy?* he wondered. *And, yet, what have I got to lose? Maybe he knows something I don't. Maybe he can help me un-screw myself. And worst case, if he turns out to be a loon, I still get a free meal out of it.*

When they ordered at the counter and sat down with their food, Peter bowed his head briefly for a moment of solitary prayer. *He's a religious nut job*, Brian thought sarcastically. Brian attended church, but he never prayed in public. *Perfect. How do I get myself into these situations?*

When Peter was done praying, he globbed ketchup on his fries. "If my wife knew I was here eating this, she'd blow a gasket. But every now and then, a man just needs some fries!"

"Have you tried fries from an air fryer? They're healthier for you."

"Yeah, and they suck, too," Peter answered. "I think air frying fries is a crime against nature. It's like caffeine-free diet soda—*why*? What's the purpose of that? If you remove all the sugar and caffeine, all you're left with is malted battery acid. It makes no sense to me. Same with removing the grease from French fries."

Brian laughed. "I think you're missing the point."

"Yeah, so my wife tells me. Again and again." He made quick work of a handful of fries and then leaned back. "Mmm-mmm-mmm. Lord, have mercy on me, a sinner." After swallowing, he picked up a few more fries. "Tell me about yourself, Brian. How many kids do you have? How long were you married, and how long have you been separated?"

Brian recounted his story as Peter ate fries. He met Bethany in college, and they had been dating for about a year when she became pregnant with Megan. Bethany refused to get married until she could fit properly into her wedding dress. After Megan was born, she couldn't lose the weight, so she kept postponing the wedding. After two years, she was pregnant with Brian Jr. At that point, she decided she wasn't going to lose it, and it was time to get married. However, things went badly from the start. They struggled through their marriage for four years, but it never really worked. They were always fighting. He loved Bethany, but he certainly did not like her anymore. And she didn't like or respect him. Then, one day, Bethany said she wanted a divorce. That was two years ago. The divorce was just finalized a few months ago.

"I'm sorry you went through that," Peter said. "You've had some tough times."

Brian shrugged. "It happens. What are you going to do?"

"Well, that's actually a very good question. What *are* you going to do now? You can't change your past, but you can change your future. So, given your current situation, what can you do about it now?"

"I thought you were going to tell me about what you learned."

"That's what I'm doing. I'm telling you the most important thing I learned."

"Which is . . . ?"

"That how you look at things largely determines how you understand your situation and what solutions you're open to. And the more perspectives you can have on your situation, the more you will come to understand where you are most vulnerable. Let me explain with a story.

Back when I was in your situation, I used to play laser tag with my kiddos. My second wife bought a laser tag set that worked in broad daylight up to about 100 yards. It was me, her, my three and her son. We would break up into teams. One team would wait in the garage with a walkie-talkie while the other team hid. When the second team was ready, they would call it in on the walkie-talkie and then the first team came out. The team with the last man standing won the round. That game was an absolute blast!"

"Literally!" Brian quipped. They both laughed.

"Well, one day we were playing, and my team was in the garage. It was me and my two youngest; my oldest was sitting this round out. We made our plan to clear out the front yard first and, if they weren't there, we would go around the side yard, then the backyard and finally into the woods. So, we went out front—nothing. We carefully made our way to the side of the house—nothing. Then we made our way through the backyard to the tree line—still nothing. My stepson was out there hiding, but he was a big lumbering kid. He stunk at hiding. He was always easy to find. And yet, this time, nothing. I stood behind a large oak before entering the woods. I kept poking my head out to try and find him. Nothing. I motioned for my team to spread out and then we entered the woods. Just a few feet into the woods and it was eerily quiet. I hate that, the absolute quiet before the engagement and everyone starts yelling.

"And then my laser tag set squawked. You could take four hits and then, on the fifth, you were out. 'I'm hit!' I called out for the benefit of my team but from where? I took a step sideways, trying to make myself a harder target to aim at. *Squawk!* I was hit again, but I still couldn't see from where. I was confused. Normally, after two hits, you know where the other person is. However, this time I couldn't see him. I took two steps to the other side. *Squawk!* The third hit, only two more before I'd be tagged out. I decided retreat was the better side of valor.

"I turned to take cover behind a large tree I had just passed when I saw him out of the corner of my eye. He was perfectly camouflaged in some undergrowth that provided him with a narrow window of fire right where I was standing. However, instead of positioning himself so he could shoot straight at us, his window of fire was at a forty-five-degree angle. I would have had to walk nearly sideways to see him. He was shooting at me as I passed him rather than when I approached him. When I stepped to one side and then the other, I stayed in his line of fire.

"I shot back, moved out of his line of fire, and positioned my team to flank him. When he got up to run, we tried to tag him out. But that's when my wife tagged me out. Then her son turned around and, together, they tagged out the rest of my team."

Brian thought about it for a moment. "That's a good story, but what does it mean?"

"My wife's strategy was not hoping my whole team would fail to see her son's hiding place. Her strategy was to position her son so he could put *me* on the defensive. Then the two of them could work as a team to tag me out. Her strategy was to beat one person—me. After tagging me out, taking care of the rest of my kiddos was easy."

Brian looked at Peter expectantly. "Okay, so . . . ?"

Peter smiled his crooked, ironic smile. "After my wife and stepson won, we walked back to the garage to start another round. On the way back, she confessed that she never cared whether she won the round or not; she just wanted to tag me out. Both she and my stepson cooked up the idea that tagging me out first was the most important thing. They considered my two youngest largely harmless in a laser-tag fight, so they concentrated on me."

Brian laughed. "Largely harmless. That's funny!"

"We didn't lose that round because they had a better plan. The fact that my stepson only tagged me three times shows how poor the execution of the plan was. Between his position and where I was standing, he had me dead to rights. He should have tagged me out in two seconds flat. Instead, he only tagged me three times. He never learned to shoot that laser-tag gun straight. We didn't lose because the other team had a better plan or better execution. We lost because I didn't know what they were really trying to accomplish. I thought they would try to tag whatever target of opportunity came their way first. Had I known they were targeting me specifically, I would have moved my team into the woods differently to provide better mutual cover and support, rather than the *flush 'em and tag 'em* approach."

"I'm still not seeing the point of this story."

Peter smiled. "The point is that if you fail to identify the real target or the real goals, you'll miss what your situation really is. Just like I missed what the real target was, you're missing what the real target is in your situation. And when that happens, well, this isn't laser tag with a stepson who can't hit the inside of a barn."

"Are you saying my ex wants to kill me?"

"I have no idea; I've never met your ex," Peter said with a smile. "But from what I saw today, she's clearly thought about it a few times!" They both laughed. "No, seriously, Brian, you're facing an enemy that already has the drop on you. You know something's wrong, but you can't see your enemy. You can't see him because you're facing the wrong direction and you're focused on the wrong things."

Brian sighed. "You're not going to tell me that my enemy is the red dude with a pitchfork, are you?"

"Oh, if only it were that simple. No, we can leave the red dude and his pitchfork behind for the moment. The enemy you need to fight is a different critter altogether."

Brian waited. Finally, he broke the silence. "Well? Are you going to tell me who he is or not?"

"Yes," Peter said, "but not today. Not yet." Peter pulled a business card from his wallet and handed it to Brian. It had his name and contact information.

Brian looked at it incredulously. "A business card? Seriously? Who uses these things anymore?"

"As much as I like my smartphone, I still think business cards have their place."

"Uh-huh," Brian grunted. He placed the card on the table, took a picture of it with his phone, and handed the card back to Peter. Peter smiled and took the card.

"Here's what I would like to do, Brian. I would like to meet with you regularly to walk you through fatherhood. Let me teach you what I learned over the years."

"Isn't that what we were supposed to do during this meal?"

"Yes, but we can only do so much over a single meal. Fatherhood is a big topic, and it can't be covered in just a couple of sessions. It needs more time than that. You need more time than that." Brian was about to protest, but Peter held up his hand. "Let me suggest we meet again in two weeks. I'll meet you here at the same time after drop-off and we can talk. We can continue to meet every other Sunday until you feel like this is no longer beneficial to you. How about it?"

"It depends."

"On what?"

"Are you really looking to help me, or are you just looking to justify your French fry habit?"

Peter laughed. "Well, let's just call it a win-win scenario. What do you say?"

"I'm interested. What would be involved?"

"Well, your visitation is every other weekend, correct?"

"Yes, and alternating holidays."

"Okay, let's do this. We'll meet here after every weekend visit for about an hour or so. But in between our visits, I want you to keep a journal."

"That sounds like homework," Brian said.

"In a sense, it is. But the goal is to get you to be a lot more intentional about your role as a father. Keeping a regular journal will allow you to focus on what you need to do. It will help you make better decisions by seeing what works and what doesn't; what was successful and what needs to be reconsidered. I did it, and I promise you it's worth your time."

"What would the journal look like?"

"If you were living with your children, I would suggest a weekly journal. In your case, every other week will work. Start it tomorrow and let it run through the next time we meet. At the beginning of the week—well, every other week—I want you to put the start date and the end date at the top. And then I want you to answer three questions. You may want to take a note of these questions."

Brian unlocked his phone and pulled up a note-taking app.

"The first question is: What are one or two ways you will spend time with your children this week? Think beyond your normal visitation schedule. If you make a video call with them, send them a text message, or even send them a card—yes, a real, physical card you buy at the store—all of that counts. Try to have regular contact with them beyond normal visitation."

"What about playing an online video game with them?"

"Absolutely, especially if you can voice chat while playing. The second question is: What are the urgent things that need to be done with your children this week? These are doctor appointments, dentist appointments, things that need to be bought, picked up, whatever. This is the day-to-day stuff that needs to happen. Look for opportunities in the day-to-day to stay involved. However, make sure it's okay with Bethany. Don't ever surprise her. Offer to help and allow her to accept your help or decline it. If she declines, be gracious and let it go. There will be many more opportunities.

"The third question is, What planned events do you have with your children this week? Check with Bethany for this one, and make sure she knows which events you want to attend. Again, no surprises."

"Yes. This sounds easy."

"That's because we're not done yet. That's what you do at the beginning of the period. At the end of the week—or, at the end of the two weeks in your case—you're going to finish your journal. You're going to answer four questions. Here they are. One, How did this week go with your children? Write down what happened in a few lines. Two, How do you feel you did this week as a father? Here, let your emotions out a bit. Some weeks are better than others. The journey of fatherhood is a journey of highs and lows. Write down the highs and lows. Third, What was your biggest win as a father? What went well? What worked out? Write it down. Finally, What didn't work out? What needs to change? Write a few lines on what you tried that failed or perhaps what you need to change. Okay, have you got all that?"

"I do." Brian punched a few more keys into his phone. "I just sent you a text so you have my number. I'll see you two weeks from today."

"I look forward to it. And bring your journal with you."

"I will."

Summary of Key Points

- How you look at things largely determines how you understand them and what solutions you are open to.

- If you fail to identify the real target or the real goals, you will miss what your situation really is.

- Be intentional with your role as a father. Use journaling to keep track of what worked and what did not. You'll be amazed by the growth you will see in your children and in your fatherhood.

2 Broken Images

G enesis 1

Two weeks later, Brian returned the children to Bethany, and this time he was only five minutes late. *Improvement!* he thought, although he knew better than to seek affirmation from his ex. As he got out of his car, Brian looked around quickly to find Peter without luck. He was anxious to meet with him. He had texted his French-fry-eating mentor to confirm their appointment, but Peter gave no clue what they would talk about today. After Bethany drove away with the children, he found Peter waiting for him in the restaurant. They ordered dinner, sat down, and once again Peter offered a silent prayer.

"So!" Peter said, globbing ketchup on his fries. "How did this weekend go?"

Brian shrugged. "About the same. Bethany texted me during the week to say that Brian Jr. was missing one of his socks. I dug down further in the air vent and found it." They both laughed.

Peter stuffed a wad of ketchup-laden fries into his mouth. His eyes fluttered, nearly rolling back into his skull. "Mmm-mmm-mmm. Lord, have mercy on me, a sinner."

"I feel like I'm watching you have a foodgasm."

Peter laughed, surprised by Brian's off-color comment. "Well, yeah, I suppose it's a lot like that. When you're a young man, food isn't all that important to you. But as you get older, it becomes crucial. Life is more about the food than when you're younger. Trust me." He held up another small handful of ketchupped fries. "Cheers!" he said and ate them with half-closed eyes and a look of pure delight on his face.

Brian held up his soda as a toast. "*Mazel tov*," he said and took a sip.

"Okay," Peter said as if he had completed the oblation offering of the first fries to God and was now ready to start their meeting. "Last time we talked about journaling. Did you bring it?"

Brian held up his phone. "I did."

"You journal on your phone? That screen is *tiny*!"

"I journal on my laptop, but I have it available on my phone." Brian tapped his screen a few times. "Here it is. I wasn't consistent at journaling. And I only got a few things done that I wanted to."

Peter nodded. "Yeah, that's normal when you're first starting out. You haven't figured out what's doable yet. Expect that in the first few months you'll bounce back and forth between planning too much and not planning enough. It takes time to find that balance."

"How long did it take you to find it?"

Peter shrugged. "Well, let's just say I'm still looking for it. Let's make sure we understand the value of planning and journaling. I believe planning is almost always useful, but plans are often worthless. You spend time developing your plan, and then something goes wrong, or something unexpected happens. I call that 'Life happens.' There's a lot of truth in the old saying: if you want to make God laugh—truly laugh—just tell him all your plans. When life happens, all your plans go out the window. Just roll with it and know that God is still working in your life. I call those moments pop quizzes from God; he just wants to know how I respond to something, whether I'll honor him or freak out. Anyway, I'm preaching. How did this week go?"

"I'm really glad you said all that. I was getting down on myself because I only did a couple of things. My plan was to reach out to Megan to play an online game with her twice a week. However, one evening she had a friend over, and another evening I lost track of time. When I remembered, Bethany said no, it was too close to bedtime."

"Does that mean you played a game with her twice before you saw them this weekend?"

"Well, yes and no. The first time we were trying to figure out the technology and the game. We had an issue with her headphones that took a while to sort out. And then we had to learn the game because it's new. By the time we got to having fun, it was time for her to go. But we played again a couple days later for about an hour. I think she enjoyed it a lot."

"Well done, Brian. And did you plan out your weekend visit?"

"Yes. It wasn't much of a plan, though. The weather yesterday was nice, so I took them to the park to play. I got to push Megan on the swing and chase Brian Jr. around, making sure he didn't eat a rock or a bug. After that, I took them to dinner, and I hope they don't tell their mother it was fast food. The dollar menu is about all I can afford. Today was the normal Sunday: church, lunch, a little downtime, and then drop-off."

Peter nodded his approval. "Not every visit needs to be planned out to the *nth* degree to be a super-spectacular, unforgettable weekend. Low-key weekends have their place. I like that you took them to the park. Playing outside is great for kids, and unstructured play time with them is even better."

"Thank you. I have a question about journaling. I looked into it online, and I saw several people say that journaling should be handwritten instead of on a computer. What do you think?"

Peter looked noncommittal. "Right now, I think it's more important that you get into the habit of journaling whatever way you can. Some people say that physically writing in your journal helps you to mentally process what you are writing. However, it takes longer to write, and an electronic journal is incredibly convenient. Stick with the way you've started for a month or two until the habit is developed. After that, try it the other way and see what you think. I hand-wrote my journal for years and then switched to electronic."

"Why?"

"Two reasons. One, I got tired of all the paper. Electronic is much more convenient and flexible. Two, I got tired of physically writing. My handwriting has always been terrible and for longer end-of-week reviews, it just got to be too much."

"What do you use for journaling?"

Peter smiled. "Well, don't laugh, but I use a program designed to write software. I write everything in markdown and then keep it organized. It allows me to keep many small files and switch between them easily. It works for me, but I'm not sure I would recommend it."

"Markdown? That's what IT folks use. It's easy to use. Good suggestion, thanks."

"I recommend it for you because you work in IT. I wouldn't recommend normal people try to use it. All right," Peter said, transitioning their discussion to what he wanted to teach. "The last time, we left off our conversation at the issue of identifying the genuine target of what you face."

"Right. You said the target isn't the guy dressed in red with a pitchfork, but that it was whoever already had the drop on me. So, who is he?"

"Well, before we get to that, we need to cover a few things. We need to look at what fatherhood was originally intended to be."

"Hold on," said Brian. "Last time, you told me you were going to tell me who I'm dealing with, and now you're telling me I'm not ready yet so let's talk about something else? This feels a little like a bait-and-switch thing."

"Well, to be exact, I told you last time that you weren't ready yet, that the subject takes time to explain, and you need more time. So that's what I want to do now. I want to give you the background you need so you can understand what you're currently facing."

"Um . . . okay, but how long will this take? I'm not sure I want to drag these meetings out forever. I mean, yeah, sure, I really enjoy watching you eat fries, but sooner or later it will get old."

Peter smiled his crooked, quizzical smile. "Trust me. I know what I'm doing." Brian got the distinct sense that what Peter was really saying was more than a blithe "you don't know what you don't know." It was more like, "You don't know to the point that you have no clue how much you don't know."

Brian sensed his own impatience rising. Rather than give into it, he decided to just take the next step with Peter's mentoring. Brian knew he needed the help. He breathed deeply, exhaled slowly, and nodded to indicate he was putting aside his impatience and was ready to learn.

Peter pulled out his Bible. "Let's start at the very beginning."

"A very good place to start," Brian sang.

Peter laughed, recognizing the reference to *The Sound of Music*. "Okay, Genesis 1."

Brian was shocked. "Oh, wow. You were being literal when you said you wanted to start at the beginning!"

"Yes, I was. In Genesis 1, God creates the world in six days, and everything he creates is good. At the end of the sixth day, he creates humans, gives them instructions, and declares that the totality of everything he created was not just good, it was very good. What I want to do today is to focus on the actual creation of humans. I want to look at the ideal state of man and woman because it is foundational to a proper understanding of fatherhood."

"Um . . ." Brian hesitated. "This looks like we're about to step into the war between the sexes."

"Yes, we are. Right into ground zero of that war. There is no way to talk about fatherhood without also talking about the relationship between men and women."

Brian looked around furtively to see who might be eavesdropping.

Peter agreed with his concern. "Yeah, I know that feeling. If we talk about this in public, someone may overhear, and a riot could break out. This topic has always been difficult and heated, but these days it's incendiary. It's nearly impossible to have the discussion without someone's head exploding. A lot of people would prefer to duck out of the conversation altogether."

"Exactly. Doesn't 'discretion is the better side of valor' make sense in this case?"

"No, not this time. If we want to understand what fatherhood was meant to be, we're going to have to confront the difficult subject of men and women head on. So, brace yourself."

Brian took a moment to resign himself to his fate. "Well, I suppose today is as good as any other to die a horrible, miserable death. I wonder if my accidental death and dismemberment policy covers this." He saw Peter's confused reaction. "My thinking is if I start by assuming a worst-case scenario, all my surprises are pleasant ones."

"Outstanding. That's the spirit, my boy; way to keep a positive attitude! Oy." Peter rolled his eyes. "Let's get started. I want to focus on Genesis 1 verses 26 through 28." Peter opened his Bible and put it on the table so they could both read it.

> 26 Then God said, "Let Us make man in Our image, according to Our likeness; and let them rule over the fish of the sea and over the birds of the sky and over the cattle and over all the earth, and over every creeping thing that creeps on the earth."

> 27 God created man in His own image, in the image of God He created him; male and female He created them.

> 28 And God blessed them; and God said to them, "Be fruitful and multiply, and fill the earth, and subdue it; and rule over the fish of the sea and over the birds of the sky, and over every living thing that moves on the earth."

"Okay, Brian, let's start with the focus on man being created in the image and likeness of God. Christians have speculated extensively about what being created in the image and likeness of God is all about. Rather than rehash all that, let me ask you to step into the shoes of the original audience for a moment. At the time Genesis was written, people believed their rulers, in this case Pharaoh, was a god and the people were created to serve the pantheon of gods. The idea was that the gods were too high and exalted for menial labor, so they created humans to do all the menial work so the gods could lounge around. This assumption was nearly universal in ancient cultures of the Near East, even though the pantheon of gods were different from place to place. People were born to be slaves of the gods—gods who cared nothing for them. People lived, served, and died. Now, the original audience of Genesis, the people of Israel, had just come out after four hundred years in Egypt, much of it as slaves. Ancient Egypt was awash in this view of humans and the gods. So, when the people of Israel heard they were created in the image of God, what would they have thought?"

"Hmm. It must have been quite a culture shock to go from a slave to a god."

"Well, let's be careful about calling them gods. Although they were created in the image of God, that doesn't make them gods."

"Why not?"

"Although this may feel like it has the language of conception, it's really about the image and likeness of God, or what theologians refer to with the Latin term *imago dei*. In ancient cultures, images were important, much more so than today. Today an image is a marketing thing for people to identify a company, like a corporate logo. When you buy a coffee and there's a green mermaid on the cup, you know what it means. When you're shopping and you see a yellow smiley face, you know what that is too. However, in ancient culture, images were something much more serious. Images were representations of people.

"Kings would often put images of themselves throughout their realm, in cities and villages. They were there to remind people who their king was. And it was to see how people treated the image."

"Isn't that vanity?" Brian asked. "I mean, putting statues of yourself everywhere? How narcissistic were these guys?"

"But it wasn't about narcissism," Peter answered. "There were practical purposes to those images. First, those images marked the territory of a king's reign. A city or village with an image was under the rule of that king. It was a reminder to the people of the government."

"Was it like flying an American flag in the middle of a small town?" Brian asked.

"Sort of, yeah. Just like we would say the Pledge of Allegiance to the flag as a way of demonstrating our acknowledgment of the federal government, so people would bow to the image of the king as a way of acknowledging his rule over them. And yet images were also more than that. You see, in the ancient world, the image was a direct representation of the thing imaged. What you did to the image you did to the king. So, when you bowed to an image, you were bowing to the king. When you showed homage to the image of the king, you were showing homage to the king himself. Does that make sense?"

Brian nodded.

"Now, a king was always concerned to know whether there were people in his kingdom ready to rebel against him. So, what he would do is erect an image in a city or town and then place a trusted agent somewhere to watch how people treated the image. If they bowed and paid homage, they were very likely loyal. However, if they failed to bow and pay homage, they failed to bow and pay homage to the king. That signaled trouble. Worse, if they spat at the image or defaced it, it was the same as spitting on and violating the king directly. This suggested that these people were ready to revolt against the king."

"That sounds like spying to me," Brian said.

"Yeah, well, maybe it will help to think of images used this way as an ancient opinion poll. 'When an image was placed in the town square, 53 percent bowed, 10 percent spat at it, and 37 percent were either neutral or not sure.'" They both laughed. Peter continued, "But let's be careful to understand images in the ancient world correctly. The primary use of images was to signify the thing represented. Or, better, they were representations of the thing signified. Therefore, what does it mean that the first man and woman were created in the image of God?"

"It means that they were created to represent God?"

"Yes. They were created to be His representatives on the earth. They were not created to *be* gods; they were created to *represent* God. Just as a king would appoint a prime minister as his representative to carry out the rule of the king, so God created the man and the woman to be His representatives on the earth. Look at verse 26: '... *let them rule over the fish of the sea and over the birds of the sky and over the cattle and over all the earth, and over every creeping thing that creeps on the earth.*' And the second half of verse 28: '... *rule over the fish of the sea and over the birds of the sky, and over every living thing that moves on the earth.*' This is the language of regency, of humans as God's ruling representative on the earth.

"Now, Brian, let me return to my original question: How do you think the original audience would have received this?"

"Well," Brian said, "it would have lifted them from abject slavery to the gods to being a ruler with God. It would be difficult to treat people poorly if they are created in the image of God."

"Yes, good."

"It must have been very empowering to know that their lives meant more than living menial existences of backbreaking work that had no real consequence."

"Absolutely."

"And it would have given them purpose and hope. I mean, if you're designated by God Himself for a role, then that's really something!"

"Very good."

"But I have a question. I was always told that being created in the image of God focused on humans having a soul and having the ability to make moral choices. What you're telling me is different."

Peter answered, "You will find Christians arguing for both interpretations. I don't think the one excludes the other. Yes, part of being created in the image of God is that we are moral beings and that we have a soul. However, by itself, I think it presents an incomplete picture. Angels are also moral beings. When some angels rebelled against God, they demonstrated they were moral beings capable of making bad moral choices. Yet we don't think of them as created in the image of God."

"I can see that," Brian said.

"There's another problem too. What about a person who is incapable of exercising morality or making moral choices? What about a person in a coma or vegetative state? Or maybe an unborn child. If the image of God is based solely on our ability to make moral choices, we would have to ask whether people in these conditions still retain the image of God. So, moral choices are a part of the image of God, but not the totality of it."

"But neither can those same people rule in God's place. If they can't rule, isn't it the same problem?"

"In the ancient world, sometimes a king would test the loyalty of his subjects. When he would select an emissary to send to them, he would choose someone who was obviously unqualified, a person with a speech defect or a mental handicap—someone folks would otherwise laugh at or dismiss. He would select someone who was so unqualified that it would seem either to be a cruel joke or that the king himself had completely lost his mind. Remember, the image represented the king so, for many people, if the image was dysfunctional, the king must be dysfunctional too. What if God also sends us people in His image who are obviously unable to fulfill their ruling duties? What if He sends us people who have mental development issues like Asperger's or autism? What if He sends us people who are so emotionally broken they are unable to form stable relationships? What if He sends us people who will always be the objects of our solicitude and charity? Do you think they might still function as the images of God?"

"Wow. I've never thought of it like that."

"I think the worst thing people do (and Christians in particular) is to dismiss the beggar or panhandler as a scammer or a lazy bum who just needs to go get a job. Yes, there are many scammers out there. But even scammers bear the image of God. I wonder how many of them have been sent by God simply to see whether we will treat them as the image bearers that they are. I don't always need to give money to a beggar on the street; in fact, money may be the wrong thing to give. But I can always treat everyone I meet as image bearers of the heavenly king, no matter their circumstances."

"Okay, wow, that's convincing."

"And it's also getting off topic. Let's get back to the subject. Look closely at verse 27: *'God created man in His own image, in the image of God He created him; male and female He created them.'* Notice that both the man and the woman bear the image of God equally. The statement of being created in God's image is repeated to make sure no one misses it; both man and woman bear the image of God. One does not bear the image more than the other; both bear it equally. One is not more equal than the other."

Brian studied verse 27 a moment before looking up. "As I'm reading this, maybe I don't need a bulletproof vest to have this discussion, do I?"

"No. Well, not yet anyway," Peter said with a mischievous smile. "We haven't finished the story yet. But let's stay in the moment; let's keep focusing on God's original plan. Look again at verse 28, the first part of it. *'And God blessed them; and God said to them, "Be fruitful and multiply, and fill the earth."'* Be fruitful and multiply. Notice that motherhood and fatherhood were baked right into God's original plan. Motherhood and fatherhood were part of what He created, part of what He would call 'very good' in verse 31. Mothers and fathers were supposed to work together in harmony to raise their children to adulthood so that they could live out their calling to be image bearers of God. In chapter 3 verse 8, we read of the Lord taking walks through the Garden. Imagine the harmony that must have existed between Adam and Eve. Whenever they would face a problem together, they didn't need to argue it out. Instead, they could just talk it over with the Lord the next time he was in the Garden. No arguments, no strife, no hidden resentments, none of the stuff that characterizes marriages today."

Brian laughed. "This is a great story, but it's not what happens in the real world. How'd we get from there to here? What happened?"

"The Fall happened. I'll skip the details of eating the forbidden fruit for now. Let's jump forward to what happened between the man and the woman. Look at chapter 3 verse 16. Adam and Eve listened to the serpent and disobeyed God. God has just judged the serpent. He now is speaking to Eve before dealing with Adam."

> To the woman He said,
> "I will greatly multiply your pain in childbirth,
> In pain you shall bring forth children;
> Yet your desire shall be for your husband,
> And he shall rule over you."

"As for the pain of childbirth, it's repeated for emphasis. God is telling her that childbirth will be painful. We're both fathers; we get what it means even if we don't experience it. It's the last two lines that are important for what happened between men and women: *'Your desire shall be for your husband, and he shall rule over you.'* What do you think that means?"

"Well, I think it means that after the agony of childbirth, the woman will still inexplicably desire her husband sexually, and her husband will insist on more sex even after she's given birth."

Peter stared at him, unsure whether to take his answer seriously or as a joke. He smiled. "Well, now I know why you're divorced."

Brian laughed. "Ouch!"

"I'm teasing. The word for desire is a generic word that does not necessarily have a sexual connotation. Whether the word means a positive desire to build up or a negative desire to tear down is unclear; it could go either way. But it's clear that God is saying that the desire of women for men will now compete with their desire for God. Prior to the Fall, Adam and Eve could keep their priorities straight. After the Fall, however, those priorities got scrambled. God is saying that women will do dumb things because their desire for men will wash out their desire for God."

"Huh." Brian began trying to formulate his thought. "So, you're saying that feminists today are actually correct when they say a woman doesn't need a man in her life."

"Not exactly. Whether an individual woman needs a man in her life is up to her. What I'm saying is that because of men, whether from a good desire to have a man in her life or a negative desire to have no men in her life at all, a woman's focus will be taken off God and put onto men. She will not look to God to define her identity. Christians understand how a radical feminist may not be focusing on God and may be looking in the wrong places for her identity. And perhaps they can also see the same thing in a wife constantly nagging her husband. But can they see the same problem of misplaced identity in a dutiful wife and homemaker who gets her identity from being a wife and homemaker, rather than from God? As Christians, our identities are supposed to come from God alone, not other people. Too often, a woman gets her identity either from the man in her life or from the lack of a man in her life. God is saying that both are equally incorrect."

"I guess I just always assumed that Christians exalt the dutiful wife and homemaker as some sort of Christian ideal," Brian said.

"In practice, they often do. And to be fair, a lot of women have been very happy living out that role, and many have done so from a position of deep faith in God. Sweeping generalizations about men and women are difficult because there are so many exceptions. The problem is that God is saying something different in Genesis. God is saying that a woman's desire for men, whether positive or negative, will take her focus off God, and she will get her identity from someone other than God."

"Wow. That's like . . ." Brian splayed his fingers out to the sides of his head, as if it were exploding.

"Well, we're not done with the mind-blowing stuff just yet. Let's look at the last part of Genesis 3:16. *'And he shall rule over you.'* I said we were heading to ground zero of the battle of the sexes; this is it right here."

"Should we have a priest give last rites or something before we continue?" Brian quipped.

Peter smiled. "No, I don't think that will be necessary. There are two issues involved here; the issue of men becoming tyrants, and the issue of men thinking that they own their wives. Both of those issues have plenty of examples in the real world, but both are abuses of what God says. I don't want to deal with the abuses; otherwise, we'd be here all day. I want to deal with what God is saying. It's this: the harmonious relationship that the man and woman previously enjoyed is now a thing of the past. It's over. Their relationship will now be marked by disagreements and all the conflict and turmoil that comes with them.

"Let me expand on this because it's important. Prior to the Fall, the man and the woman were in the garden as equals. One did not impose his or her will on the other; both had equal access to God and could talk directly with Him. There was no sin, so there was no selfishness. Each looked out for the other. Whenever they had a disagreement, they had direct face-to-face access to God. They could ask Him and get an immediate answer. With that answer, they could resolve their difference in the light of God's clearly revealed will for the two of them and get on with things.

"After the Fall, the number-one challenge humans face is determining the will of God. It is a constant issue not just in the Bible, but in all of human history. In the Bible, people did all sorts of things to determine the will of God. They would lay a fleece before the Lord, use extispicy, omens, astrology, and they sought wisdom from the prophets."

"Aren't we just supposed to pray?"

"Yes. But how many times have we prayed and not gotten a clear answer? How many times have we prayed but really all we wanted was for God to approve the decision we had already made? How many times have we prayed for the wrong thing? Sometimes we pray fervently, yet God seems distant. Now, please don't take what I'm saying as a lack of faith. The reality is that because of the Fall, we don't have the same face-to-face presence with the Lord. Therefore, determining His will is difficult, and it is often *very* difficult."

"Amen to that," Brian said.

"What God is saying here is that when disagreements arise between the couple and a resolution cannot be found through praying together, someone will need to make a final decision. God is saying that the responsibility for the final decision rests with the husband."

"Wait a minute. Even if they disagree, shouldn't they work together to come to some sort of compromise? Shouldn't they seek a win-win solution?"

"In most circumstances, absolutely. But what about circumstances when no compromise is available? For example, let's take a hypothetical example. Say a married couple lives in Annapolis, Maryland. Both have family in Annapolis, deep friendships there, and have been attending the same church for ten years. One day, he gets a once-in-a-lifetime job opportunity in Seattle. It's one of those opportunities he simply cannot say no to. She, however, thinks uprooting the family is a terrible idea. She doesn't want to leave friends and family, and she doesn't think changing school systems is good for the children. She thinks moving to Seattle is a bad idea. The choice here is clear: move from Annapolis to Seattle or not. What would a compromise be? Move to Missouri instead? Hardly.

"Here's another example. Say a couple has a dog. The dog is getting on in years and has serious health issues. The wife wants to keep caring for the dog and do everything possible to extend his life. The husband, however, thinks continuing his life is cruel and merely extending his suffering unnecessarily. He wants to have the dog put down. What's the compromise? There isn't one."

"Yeah, but aren't these extreme examples?" Brian said. "People don't experience these sorts of things in their day-to-day lives. Shouldn't we focus on the everyday experiences rather than these extremes?"

"My point is that couples always face decisions in which there is either no compromise or one that is a compromise in name only. When that happens, who has the responsibility for making the final decision?"

"Well, they're adults. They can decide for themselves who makes the final decision. It seems arbitrary for God to decide that the man should always have the final say."

"If it were a mere person who decides for all people, then, yes, that would be an arbitrary decision. But when it is the creator of the world who decides, it's not arbitrary or unfair: it's reality."

"Yeah, but . . ." Brian started to object but was lost for words.

"Look, Brian. The real issue of the Fall was not eating a piece of forbidden fruit. If that was all that was at stake, then God's condemnation of their actions would be completely over the top and unjust. But the fruit was not the real issue. The real issue was the rejection of God's authority over them. They wanted to run their own lives, do things their own way. They didn't want to believe that His rules were for their own benefit. Instead, they thought God was holding back the good life from them with His authority, so they threw off His authority. And it's been that way ever since. When people have issues with the husband having the final say in the home, they're not having issues with the church; they're continuing the rebellion of Adam and Eve against God's authority. Either we live under God's authority, or we throw it off. Either we submit or we rebel. That's it. On this issue, there is no middle ground, and there is no third option."

"Okay," Brian challenged. "Let me give you a scenario. A husband and wife are expecting their third child. During this pregnancy, her blood pressure is sky high. The doctor puts her on bed rest and takes other measures, but nothing works. The doctor thinks the pregnancy should be terminated because she probably will not survive it. The wife is strongly pro-life; she wants to continue with the pregnancy. To her mind, she can show her baby no greater love than to lay her life down for her child. On the other hand, the husband wants to terminate. He tells her that both he and the other children need her. And in a worst-case scenario, he will be left with an infant, two small children, no wife, and a funeral. Are you saying that God has given the husband the authority to terminate the pregnancy?"

"No," Peter answered firmly. "The husband's authority does not extend to the point that he can force his wife to do anything that is either contrary to God's Word or against his wife's conscience. In this scenario, the wife's conscience would be violated if she aborted. Remember, although the husband has the responsibility for the final decision, that doesn't mean he should always use it. In this case, given the gravity of the situation, he needs to consider carefully what his wife would be justified to do if he attempted to force her to terminate. If she promptly left him, who would blame her? She is still a full image bearer of God; forcing her to do something against a deeply held belief of conscience is a very serious violation of who God created her to be."

"So, are you saying that it's the wife's body and she can do with it as she pleases?"

"No. 1 Corinthians 7:4 says, '*The wife does not have authority over her own body, but the husband does; and likewise, also the husband does not have authority over his own body, but the wife does.*' This is the language of mutual submission. The issue is that the authority of one spouse over the other's is not absolute; there are limits. Issues involving deeply held beliefs of conscience are an important boundary."

Brian furrowed his brow. "Hang on. A moment ago, you gave the example of the dog and the conflict about when to put him down. In that case, you said the husband had final say. But what if the wife's position is a deeply held belief? It's not unreasonable to say that she would have a deeply held belief not to put an animal down too quickly. It sounds to me like you're saying the husband has final say except when he doesn't."

Peter smiled. "Well done, Brian. You're listening closely. And you bring up a good point. Frankly, I don't think there is a definitive answer here. I would say that in this case, the husband should step aside. Letting the dog live is a decision that can be reversed, whereas once the dog is put down, that decision cannot be undone. But that is my thinking, not God's. I want to be careful not to put words in God's mouth. There are times and difficult situations where definitive 'Thus saith the Lord' answers are not possible. I think this is one of them. Also, in the previous hypothetical situation about moving to Seattle, it's possible the wife may have a deeply held conviction about staying close to family. To be honest, I'm not sure what the answer is. Those are the situations couples often face in which there is no compromise. Someone needs to have final say, yet without granting that person arbitrary power over the other. It's very difficult. It's a lot more difficult when one or both partners is not genuinely seeking God's guidance."

Brian's lips were pursed in thought. After a moment, he said, "Earlier you said that man and woman were created equally. Men did not dominate women. Why shouldn't we go back to that original state of equality and get rid of male patriarchy?"

"I think that many wives and mothers are trying to do just that, to get back to that original state. And I think one of the benefits has been to recognize that what God said about the husband's rulership got taken way too far. It has justified ungodly leadership both in the home and in the workplace. For example, where did God say women should be excluded from the workforce, or from certain fields of work like medicine or academia, simply because they were women? If they can do the job, and they want to do it, more power to them. There was only a single carve-out for men only, and that's the priesthood. Beyond that, have at it, ladies.

"However, God has made it clear that between the Fall and the return of Jesus, the original state Adam and Eve experienced is gone. The Fall changed us, and we can't go back. At the end of history when Jesus sets up his forever kingdom, the original equality will return. But between the Fall and that future time, we live in a different reality. In this reality, there will be differences of opinion and disagreements in our homes.

"What can be worked out through compromise should be worked out. But in the end, someone must have final say in every relationship, and marriage is no exception. God has given that role to men. The Hebrew word translated as 'rule' in Genesis 3:16 is a neutral term. It doesn't mean a tyrant or an autocratic ruler who abuses his power. It's a term that could easily be used for, say, a supervisor at work or even a principal at a school. Husbands have not been given permission by God to be tyrants or selfish jerks; there are limits to their authority. If some men turn around and abuse that responsibility, that's on them, not on what God said. If other men wimp out and disengage, that's also on them. Those are the abuses of what God has declared. We should look at the way things are supposed to be before we look at the abuses."

"This is hard stuff," Brian said, looking down.

"It is," Peter agreed. "And it gets harder before it gets better. If you think being a husband is a mess because of the Fall, being a father is an absolute train wreck. And as we continue reading what God said in Genesis 3, we see that it was more than just the male–female relationships that got confused in the Fall. It involved the totality of human relationships. Every human relationship and endeavor has been affected. We see the way things are supposed to work, but they don't. We see how government is supposed to work, but it hardly ever does. It's not because the wrong set of people is in charge; it's because of the Fall that things don't work correctly. We see the way work is supposed to be, but it rarely is. Work is often frustrating, pointless, and provides no meaning or satisfaction like it is supposed to. The Fall even affects our relationship with the earth. The earth was given to us to provide for our needs, and yet everything we do seems to screw up the environment. We see the way weather is supposed to work, but so often it doesn't. We get droughts, hurricanes, heat blasts, and ice ages. The totality of creation exhibits intricate design and planning, and yet so often it just doesn't work correctly."

"Are you saying God designed things poorly?"

"No, I'm saying the creation is cursed because of the Fall. Take a look at the next verse, Genesis 3:17."

> Then to Adam He said, "Because you have listened to the voice of your wife and have eaten from the tree about which I commanded you, saying, 'You shall not eat from it'; Cursed is the ground because of you;
>
> In toil you shall eat of it
>
> All the days of your life."

"Focus on the phrase *'Cursed is the ground.'* The ground is the very thing Adam relies on to provide life. Humans depend on the ground to provide almost everything we need for life. Originally, the earth would offer its abundance without back-breaking work. Now, because of the curse, it will only give up its abundance through very hard and often frustrating labor."

"Oh, good, I'm glad you said all that," Brian said drily. "I was afraid you might say something positive to lift me up and make me feel better."

Peter was quickly learning to appreciate Brian's satirical humor. "You bring up a good point. I don't want to leave things here until we meet again. I've given you a lot of bad news. However, let me give you some of the good news. The two verses we've just read need to be set into their proper context. Look at Genesis 3:15. God has just spoken to the serpent; now he is talking to Satan."

"I thought you said the issue isn't the red guy with the pitchfork," Brian interjected.

"It's not . . . well, not directly. But what God says is important for our discussion. Look at what He says."

> And I will put enmity
> Between you and the woman,
> And between your seed and her seed;
> He shall bruise you on the head,
> And you shall bruise him on the heel.

"The last two lines are an image familiar to people who deal with snakes. If you stomp on the head of a snake without wearing shoes, the curved teeth of the snake can point upward and pierce your heel. When you do that, you kill the snake, but you've been injured in the process, and chances are you have received the venom of the snake. With that in mind, let's look at the promise God gives in this verse. God says that there will be enmity between Satan and the woman. What is enmity?"

"Fighting?"

"Partly. It's opposition, a state of hostility that may or may not include fighting. One doesn't like the other. God is saying that hostility will not just exist between Satan and Eve, but between his seed and her seed. What do you think that means?"

Brian thought about it. "Well, I guess it means between Satan's children and Eve's children. So, maybe the demons and Eve's children?"

"Well, you're going down the right path. When God told Adam and Eve not to eat the fruit of the tree, what was the penalty supposed to be?"

"Death."

"Right. But now that she's done that, God is talking about Eve's children. What happened to the death penalty? It's been delayed. Death is now a reality for humanity, but it is not immediate. Adam and Eve will have the opportunity to bear children and raise a family. Although life on the earth will be hard, there will also be aspects of life that will be good and beautiful. I call these aspects echoes of Eden, those moments that remind us of what once was and what will be again. Those are the moments that make life so special. In other words, even before God hands down his judgment on Adam and Eve, they know that it will be mixed with mercy and grace; mercy because they will not die immediately, and grace because they will have a chance to live and raise a family even though God should have executed them on the spot. Adam and Eve have received mercy and grace, and they know it.

"What God is saying is that from all the descendants of Adam and Eve, all will be affected by the Fall. All will be tempted like Eve. The only difference is that while Eve was created in a state of innocence, her children will not be. They will be born corrupted; they will be born predisposed to rebel against God. Those are the seeds of Satan. However, just like Eve, there will be some who receive the mercy and grace of God. There will be those who sense the weight of their sin and cry out to God for mercy and grace; God's promise is that they will receive it just as Eve has received mercy and grace. And just like Eve didn't deserve it, neither will they. But God is demonstrating that even in His severity, one can still find mercy and grace with Him."

"Okay, but then it says, *'He shall bruise you on the head.'* That's a singular person, not a group of people. What's going on with that?"

"What's going on is a double-entendre. The Hebrew word for seed is both singular and plural, just like it is in English. If I say, 'I have seed,' it can mean I have an individual seed, or it can mean I have numerous seed. So, God is referring at first to numerous seed, the descendants of Eve. It's plural. And then he shifts to a singular seed, one man. One is coming who will stomp Satan out. *'He shall bruise you on the head'* is the image of a man crushing a snake's head with his heel. However, *'and you shall bruise him on the heel'* is the image of the man taking the venom of the snake to himself to defeat the snake. Does any of this sound familiar?"

Brian stared at him blankly.

"This is the promise of Jesus. One day one of Eve's descendants will take the penalty of rebellion against God to himself, and in doing that, the curse of that rebellion will be removed. That's the gospel. That's exactly what Jesus came to do."

"So . . . you got all that out of one verse?" Brian asked incredulously.

"No, I'm skipping over a lot of other Scriptural references to summarize. Our time is running short, and if we pursue this too far, it will take us away from our topic of fatherhood."

"Okay, then you bring up a good point. What has the promise of Jesus got to do with fatherhood?"

"Well, there are multiple ways to answer that question. I'm sure I'll eventually get to all of them as we continue to meet. However, for the sake of time, let me say this. The entire book of Genesis can be read from the perspective of fatherhood. From that perspective, Genesis recounts the Fall and redemption of fatherhood. What Adam has broken we see partially restored in the person of Israel. However, *redemption* might be too strong a word because the full redemption of fatherhood will come much later than Genesis. Look at the last two verses of the Old Testament. Malachi 4:5–6." Peter flipped the pages in his Bible so they could both read it.

> 5 Behold, I am going to send you Elijah the prophet before the coming of the great and terrible day of the LORD.

> 6 And he will restore the hearts of the fathers to their children, and the hearts of the children to their fathers, lest I come and smite the land with a curse.

Brian read that and remembered the forced hugs at the end of each visit with his children. His heart ached a little. What he wanted more than anything was for the hearts of his children to be turned back to him.

Peter continued, "At the end of the Old Testament, there is still friction between fathers and their children. And notice, it's not just the fathers who are a problem; so are the children. All relationships have been affected by the Fall. But the promise is that as part of Jesus's appearance, God will send a messenger who will begin to turn the hearts of fathers and their children back to each other. We learn later that the messenger is John the Baptist. His ministry will point the way to Jesus's ministry. Between them, the enmity that characterized the relationships between fathers and their children will start to unwind. People's hearts will be changed—genuinely changed—so that fathers and children will approximate what was originally intended. We won't get back to total innocence in this time between the Fall and Jesus's forever kingdom, but we can approximate it. And that's why I began at the very beginning. It's more than just a very good place to start; it puts our situation into perspective within the larger drama of God and humanity."

"I . . . uh . . . I never connected my weekend visits with the kids with God and humanity before. This is deep."

"It is. Don't feel under pressure to try and understand all this at once. It takes time. I've skipped over a lot partly for the sake of time, and partly because it's impossible to get it all at once."

There was a pause while Brian thought. He was processing everything as best he could when he finally remembered a point he wanted to return to. "I have two questions. First, why are you telling me all this? I'm divorced. This stuff about husbands and wives doesn't apply to me."

"Being a husband may not apply to you at this moment, but you don't know where you're going to be in five years. Who knows who you will meet? It's important to think about these things *before* you meet her. When you do, your head will spin, your heart will flutter, and that's the wrong time to think clearly. Also, as a husband, your role bleeds naturally into your role as a father, making it a natural starting point for any discussion of fatherhood."

"Okay. You said a minute ago that the priesthood is for men only. Why?"

"That is a great question," Peter said, checking his watch and registering shock. "But it is a very big topic. In fact, it's an important part of what we will cover next time. But my time today is just about over. I need to get back home. Before I go, let me leave you with some homework. I'm going to ask you two questions. Think about them during the next two weeks, and when we meet again, give me your answers. Sound good?"

"Sure."

"Okay. The first question involves a scenario that may seem a little macabre, but go with it. Imagine for a moment you are a spectator at your own funeral. You've lived your life, you've died, and now people are gathering for your funeral. Both of your kids will speak at your funeral. Question number one is this: What would you want your children to say about you? How do you want your children to remember you after you're gone?"

"Whoa, that's a heavy question!"

"It is. When it comes to fatherhood, it is the bottom-line question, isn't it? Fatherhood boils down to how your children will remember you. Now, if the first question is heavy, the second is gut-wrenching. The second question is this: How will you live your life so that your children will eulogize you as you want without having to lie?"

Brian exhaled. "Um . . . wow."

"Yeah," Peter agreed. "So many men stumble through fatherhood hoping to be a good father, but they have no idea what that actually means. They don't know what they're aiming at, so they have no idea if they hit the target or not. Most men are lost when it comes to fatherhood, and in the end, they settle for good enough. They may not have been the best, but they weren't terrible either. I'm not naïve; not all men can be great fathers. But I am firmly convinced that by the grace of God, all men can be positive influences in the lives of their children, even the men who have made grave mistakes in their relationships with their children. For some men, their previous mistakes are such that their positive influence will be limited. For others, they have the opportunity to really shape their children in a very positive way. The depth and breadth of the opportunities vary between situations, but all men can have a positive influence in their children's lives."

"Even men in prison?" Brian asked, half challenging and half mischievously.

Peter seemed to miss the joke entirely. "Yes, of course." He waited to see if Brian would object. "There's one more thing before I go. I said I would tell you the genuine target that you face. Perhaps it's better to ask who is targeting you. Can you guess who that is now?"

Brian's mind raced through the entire discussion, from the creation of the man and the woman to their innocent state, then to the Fall and the subsequent judgment. Nothing. And then he remembered the promise of the conflict between Eve's seed and Satan's. That was a reference to the children of Adam and Eve, all of humanity, who are born already predisposed to sin. All are tempted and fall into rebellion against God just as Eve did, but some will throw themselves on the mercy and grace of God. Brian hesitated a moment before answering, "Is it me?"

"Yes," Peter exclaimed, "that's absolutely correct—it's you! You are both the target and the one targeting you."

"So, Bethany is right; I really am my own worst enemy."

"Yes, you are. However, in God, there is always the hope of something better. The question is, will you receive God's mercy and grace, or will you keep going down the path you've been on and just hope it all works out in the end? It should be a no-brainer, but it's shocking how many men choose to ignore God and just hope for the best." Peter checked his watch again with a start. "Oh, I really need to go now. See you in two weeks?"

Brian's mind had been reeling, but he was suddenly brought back to the moment. "Yeah, I look forward to it."

"Don't forget the two questions. First, what would you want your children to say about you at your funeral? And second, how will you live your life so that your children will eulogize you as you want without having to lie?"

Summary of Key Points

- The ideal state of man and woman is foundational to a proper understanding of fatherhood.

- Images in the time of the Bible represented the extent of a king's reign and authority.

- What you did to an image, you did to the one the image represented.

- Adam and Eve were created to represent God.

- Because of the Fall, a woman's desire is taken off God and focused on men, regardless of whether it is a good desire or a bad one.

- After the Fall, the number-one challenge humans face is determining the will of God.

- When the creator of the world decides something, it is neither arbitrary nor unfair; it is reality.

3 Prophet, Priest, and King

Genesis 2

Two weeks later, Brian pulled up to the restaurant. This time he was ten minutes early. While he waited for Bethany, Peter arrived. They waved at each other, and Peter went into the restaurant. Bethany arrived a few minutes later and was surprised to see him there already. They went through the drop-off routine, including forced hugs and goodbyes, and she left.

"I see you were early this time," Peter said when they sat down with their food.

"Yeah, I was determined to be on time. So instead of trying to leave on time, I made it a point to leave twenty minutes early."

"But you arrived only a few minutes early?"

Brian laughed. "Yeah."

"Meh, that's about right," Peter said with a grin. He bowed his head in silent prayer, then opened ketchup packets to glob up his fries. Brian watched the French fry ritual all the way through to "Mmm-mmm-mmm. Lord, have mercy on me, a sinner."

"From now until the ages of ages, amen," Brian quipped.

Peter appreciated Brian's sense of humor. "Yeah, yeah. Everyone's a comedian."

Brian opened the sauce for his chicken fingers. "So, what do you have for me today?"

"Last time we met we ended our discussion with two questions. Do you remember them?"

"How could I forget? They've been on my mind for two weeks. The first question was what would I want my children to say about me at my funeral? And the second question was how will I live my life so that my children will eulogize me as I want without having to lie?"

"Good," Peter said. "Now before I ask, let me say that your answers to these questions will probably change as we continue meeting. Your initial answers are just that: initial answers. You're not locked into them. They are not set in stone. So, what is your initial answer to the first question?"

"It's great to hear that you only want an initial answer today. To be honest, at first, I thought the question was simple—almost simplistic. But the more I tried to answer it, the harder the question became. So, my initial answer is that I want my children to remember me as a good father, someone who really loved them and tried his best to do right by them." Brian stopped, unsure how his response sounded.

"That's a good start," Peter said. "It shows your heart is in the right place. As we continue, you will add more to it, and you will make it more specific. I don't think you have enough in your answer to start answering the second question yet, but your first answer is on the right track. As we keep exploring fatherhood, you will have more opportunities to flesh out your answer. In fact, today's discussion should give you a lot you can use. And it should help you to start thinking about how you will live your answer out."

"I'm all ears," Brian said eagerly.

"Hang on. Before we start, tell me about your journaling over the past two weeks."

"Oh, right." Brian pulled out his phone and swiped a few times. "Here it is. It wasn't much this week. I planned on playing an online game with Megan twice instead of four times, but one of the times didn't work out. I forgot to put it on my calendar, so I missed the window. But the time we played was fun. It was the same game. She had been practicing, so she mopped the floor with me."

Peter laughed. "Good girl!"

"Yeah. And then I sent both of my kids a card letting them know I was thinking of them. I doubt Brian Jr. understood it, but it keeps me on his radar, so to speak."

"It does. Well done. I like that you're beginning to think about ways you can connect with your kids even when you can't be physically present with them. Keep working on that. I know it takes effort, but those are the little things that really pay off in the long run. All right," Peter said, transitioning the conversation to what he wanted to teach. "Last time we looked at the creation of man and woman and what happened with them. They were created as bearing the image of God to live with God in harmony. However, the image was broken because of the Fall, and the result was disunity and strife between the man and the woman, a situation that has been passed down through the human race ever since.

"What I want to do today is to dig deeper into the original state of Adam. I want us to see God's plan more closely so we can more accurately understand what God's intention for fathers was supposed to be. To do that, we need to approach the book of Genesis correctly. In the twenty-first century, we approach the creation account either from a scientific perspective or from the point of view of history as we understand good history today. However, the original audience was a prescientific people, and they had different standards for what counted as good history. This is not to denigrate them or say they were dumb. They weren't. In fact, they could be quite intelligent. However, they simply did not have the tools available to them to understand creation the way we can today, so science was not a primary concern for them. Nor were they concerned with a history that was a dry recitation of the facts. When we read Genesis, it's important to step into their shoes, so to speak, and see the world from their perspective rather than from a twenty-first-century one. We must always remember the original audience of the book of Genesis. When it was penned, there was a specific group of people the author was writing to. The author was writing for that group to understand it. If we are going to understand what the author intended, we need to read it through the eyes of the original audience."

"Was their perspective all that different from ours?" Brian asked.

"It was. In fact, it was very different. Not only were they a prescientific people, but their social and political structures were completely different from the West. If we fail to see Genesis through their eyes, then we will miss what it's trying to tell us. And that is especially true when it comes to fatherhood.

"In Genesis 1, the creation of the man and woman is recounted in summary form. Think of it as the author saying, 'Look at what creation looked like from a high level.' In Genesis 2, the author shifts the vantage point from up above to down in it. He's taking the reader from up above it all and putting his metaphorical boots on the ground. He wants the reader to see more detail about the creation of the man and the woman."

Peter placed his Bible on the table between them. "Let's start with Genesis 2:7. *'Then the LORD God formed man of dust from the ground and breathed into his nostrils the breath of life; and man became a living being.'* Now, notice that at the end of chapter 1, God had already created both Adam and Eve. But here in chapter 2, the author has taken us back to the creation of Adam. Eve has not been created yet."

"I've heard people say that Genesis had two different creation accounts. Is that wrong?"

"Probably. Genesis provides two accounts of the same event told from two different perspectives. The first account was a high-level summary of what happened, as if the reader was hovering way up above everything. It's the perspective of God. In chapter 2, the author moves his audience into the middle of things. This is more of the human view, even while the author gives us an omniscient narration."

"Wait a minute," Brian objected, "I heard that Genesis was put together by different people, and that's what accounts for the different creation stories. Different writers wrote the various stories, and someone blended them together into the book of Genesis."

"Well, the technical term for putting different stories together is *redaction*. Some people believe there were four major editors who took stories from the societies around them and redacted them until the Bible was put into its final form. The different points of view between Genesis 1 and 2 are used as evidence of the editor stitching different stories together. Now, let's assume that's true for a moment. I'm not saying it is or it isn't; let's just assume it's true. My question is simple: Did the editors bother to proofread what they wrote? Or did they just throw the rough draft over the fence and say, 'Ta-da! Here's your book of origins!' Given the influence the book of Genesis has had on history, that seems far-fetched to me. I think it's better to believe that the editors *did* proofread it, and that the shift in perspectives was intentional. Otherwise, these guys were horrible editors."

"I've never thought of it that way," Brian said. "Yeah, it makes sense that the editors would have proofread their work and gotten rid of obvious errors."

"Okay, so let's get back to the story. The author has moved the narration so the reader can see what is going on. Adam has been created, but not Eve. Now, look at verse 8. *The LORD God planted a garden toward the east, in Eden; and there He placed the man whom He had formed.'* The next time we meet, we'll look more closely at what this Garden would have meant to the original audience. For now, I just want to set the stage for what is going on. Adam has been created as well as the Garden, and God placed the man in the Garden. In verses 9 through 14, the narrator goes on a detour, but he returns to Adam and the Garden in verse 15."

15 Then the LORD God took the man and put him into the garden of Eden to cultivate it and keep it.

16 The LORD God commanded the man, saying, "From any tree of the garden you may eat freely;

17 but from the tree of the knowledge of good and evil you shall not eat, for in the day that you eat from it you shall surely die."

"God created both Adam and the Garden, placed Adam into the Garden, and then gave him instructions. He is to cultivate and keep the garden, he may eat freely from whatever the Garden produces. There is only one thing he cannot do; he cannot eat the fruit from one particular tree."

"That seems like a simple set of instructions."

"It is. But something is missing. We're getting to the reason why God created humans male and female as we read in chapter 1."

18 Then the LORD God said, "It is not good for the man to be alone; I will make him a helper suitable for him."

"The word *suitable* means standing face-to-face with him, Adam's equal. God is saying that Adam needs someone to help him in his work of cultivating and keeping the Garden. And so, what happens? Look at verses 19 and 20."

19 Out of the ground the LORD God formed every beast of the field and every bird of the sky, and brought them to the man to see what he would call them; and whatever the man called a living creature, that was its name.

20 The man gave names to all the cattle, and to the birds of
the sky, and to every beast of the field, but for Adam there
was not found a helper suitable for him.

"Okay, Brian, here's my question for you. If it wasn't good for
Adam to be alone, why didn't God create Eve at the same time as
Adam? Why is God going through all of this?"

"Um . . ." Brian thought about it for a moment and finally shrugged
his shoulders.

"God already knew that Adam would need a helper. Now he wants
Adam to recognize that same need. He wanted Adam to come to the
same conclusion on his own. Now, pay close attention to the order of
events. In verse 18, God already determined to make him a helper. So,
why does he parade all the critters before Adam so he can name them
before making Eve?"

"So that Adam can name them?"

"Adam could have named them at any time—why does he do that
now, between God's pronouncement to make Adam a helper and
actually making his helper?"

"Was it so Adam could see that the other animals were not good
helpers for him?"

"Yes, exactly. God wanted Adam to recognize that no other
creature was his perfect helper; only the woman was his perfect mate.
God does this to get Adam to recognize his own need. In other words,
rather than just springing the woman on him, he first takes the time to
let Adam see his need. God is showing Adam what a loving father does.
Rather than just provide a solution to his child's problem, he takes the
time to encourage his child to explore a problem. He lets the child work
out as much of it as he can."

Brian looked sheepish. "Yeah, I don't do that. I get impatient and
just solve the problem for my kids."

"Don't be embarrassed; a lot of parents do that. But from now on, try to let your kiddos figure their problems out whenever you can. Be patient; take the time with them just as God took the time with Adam. And when you think about how long it takes, remember how long it took Adam to name all the creatures. It probably wasn't quick and easy."

"Patience is hard," Brian said, remembering several times when his impatience caused him to snap at his children.

"It is. Just remember that you're not alone. All fathers go through the pain of learning patience, and no one ever learns it quickly or easily. Patience comes in stages, not all at once."

"Okay," Brian said, feeling a little better.

"Now," Peter continued, "remember I said we need to read this as the original audience would have read it. What I want to do next is to fill in some of the details that the original audience would have seized on. The first detail is Adam naming the animals. Modern readers miss the significance of this because today the name given to an animal is given by the scientist or scientists who first discover it. But remember that the original audience was a prescientific people. In their world, to name something was to exercise authority over it. Just as a father demonstrates his authority over his child by selecting the child's name, so Adam was demonstrating his authority over the animals by naming them."

"Well, hang on. There's another way of looking at this," Brian said. "This could just be that Adam has a larger brain and is capable of communication. Naming them is just showing he's more highly evolved than the other critters."

"Yes," Peter responded, "that's how we might read it *today*. However, it's unlikely the original audience would have read it that way. We always need to keep how the original audience would have read it in mind. Otherwise, we will make the text say things the author never intended to say. We put words into the author's mouth." Brian nodded in understanding.

Peter continued, "The point about Adam naming the animals is that no other animal demonstrates authority over another animal. Even angels were not given this authority. Only Adam had it. Now, when I mention authority, who do you think of when you think about people in authority?"

"Well, my boss at work," Brian answered. "The owner of my company."

"Think about authority in the sense of ruling, having control over."

"Um, well, the president. Oh, wait, they didn't have a president. So, would this be a king?"

"Yes, exactly. A king. When Adam names the animals, he is exercising a kingly role. The original audience would have understood the imagery. But there's more to this kingly imagery than just naming the animals. Look back again at verse 15. *Then the LORD God took the man and put him into the garden of Eden to cultivate it and keep it.*' When God put Adam into the Garden, it was with a purpose: to cultivate it and to keep it. Let's focus on the two purposes of cultivating and keeping because they are important. First, what comes to mind when you see that Adam is supposed to cultivate the Garden?"

Brian's brow furrowed. "To me, it means maintaining a garden. Tilling the ground and, I don't know, growing plants and stuff."

Peter smiled. "You're not a gardener, are you?"

"Not really, no."

"That's fine. We'll get into the full imagery of the Garden next time we meet. For now, know that the Garden was meant to do triple duty: It was Adam's home, it was where he would grow the food he needed to eat, and it was the place where he would meet with God. Almost everything that happens in and around the Garden has to do with one of those three things. So, the next question is, when God calls on Adam to cultivate the Garden, is this an issue with Adam's home, his food production, or meeting God?"

"Growing food," Brian answered.

"Correct. Now, focus on the second command, to keep the Garden. The Hebrew word *shamar* is a military term. It means to keep in the sense of a soldier standing guard or securing something. It's making an area safe. It means that Adam was supposed to protect the Garden from those who would enter to defile it. Adam's first purpose in the Garden was to grow food to provide for his family. Remember, the last time we met, we saw that family was baked right into his original creation. The command to cultivate the Garden is a picture of Adam providing food. Second, he was to make sure the Garden was safe from those who would defile or despoil the Garden.

"For the original audience, these two commands would have described the roles of a king. A king had three important functions in their day: to provide, to protect, and to rule. A king was supposed to provide prosperity, the things people needed to live a good life. He was supposed to protect his subjects from invaders and those who would seek to do them harm. And, finally, he was to rule, to exercise authority through establishing laws, to set the rules so that people knew what was expected of them. All three of the kingly duties are present in what God commands Adam to do."

"Wow, I've never seen this before! Um . . . are you saying that Adam was a king?"

"Sort of. Adam definitely had kingly responsibilities. He had the responsibility to provide for his home, to protect it, and to establish just rules for his family. And that is something that is true of all men. They are to provide, protect, and establish just rules."

Brian smiled. "I'm a king? I'm supposed to rule? Sweet! Do I get a turkey leg like Henry VIII?" Brian's smile turned mischievous. "Do I get to lop off the head of my ex?"

Peter sighed with a smile. "Yeah, sorry to pop your bubble, Big Guy, but biblical kingship isn't like that. The Bible limits a king's authority.[2] He is not to be a tyrant who indulges his every whim. Kings are held accountable for their actions.[3] Kings are to rule wisely and execute justice.[4] So, slow your roll. Fulfilling a kingly role in the home is not a license for you to indulge your selfish whims. It's quite the opposite. It means that you live sacrificially for your subjects and are willing to lay down your life to protect them. It means that you do what it takes to ensure *they* are provided for rather than that *you* are provided for. And, finally, it means you sacrifice your personal wishes to provide an emotionally healthy home. A man's provision for his family is more than physical needs.[5] He is to love his wife as Christ loves the church,[6] and just to pile on, he is to provide for his extended household too.[7] It's not enough to just bring home a paycheck. He is to provide an emotionally healthy environment where positive relationships are possible."

"Wow. When you said men were kings of the home, I thought I was going to get to rule. But this is something else. I thought being a king was going to be cool, but the way you describe it, it kinda sucks."

"Brian, always be careful what assumptions you bring to the Bible. You heard 'king' and you immediately assumed you would get to do whatever you wanted. But when presented with the full biblical picture of what a king is supposed to be, you're disappointed. Why? Because when the Bible describes what a king is supposed to be, it exposes what is really in your heart: selfishness. God wasn't calling Adam to selfishness, nor is He calling you to live selfishly. He calls men to live for something more than themselves."

"So, God calls on men to live for their families?" Brian asked.

"Yes and no. First and foremost, God calls on men to live for God. It's not like God gave Adam a kingly role and left him to figure it out for himself. God gave Adam a kingly role as a picture of God's rulership over the world. As men and fathers, we may have kingly roles to fulfill, but we are still subjects of the true king. And our lives are supposed to reflect that. Our lives are supposed to reflect the love and provision and goodness of the king we serve. We are supposed to live for God first and family second. Or maybe it's better to say that the best way to fulfill your responsibilities to your family is to live for God first."

There was a pause in the conversation as Brian reflected on what Peter had said. Finally, he smiled and said, "I don't know. I think I like my version of being a king more than I like yours."

"I'm sure you do," Peter said, unimpressed. "So, tell me, Your Majesty, how's your version of being a king working out for you? Is your kingdom at home everything you hoped for?"

Brian knew he had led with his chin. "Ow. You fight dirty."

"It's not fighting dirty to point out the painfully obvious."

Brian sighed and slumped in his chair in an exaggerated fashion. Then he laughed at the absurd position he had talked himself into. "Well, I certainly hope all our meetings together will be this positive and uplifting."

"Eh," Peter said with a shrug. "This is about normal. The first thing most guys need is to have their assumptions and preconceived notions of manhood knocked down. That's the hard part. Once you've been knocked down you can be built back up. But I want to build you back up the right way, the way God always intended you to be."

Brian hesitated and considered what Peter said. He realized that there would be many hard truths yet to come, truths that would probably be very uncomfortable. It would be easy enough to leave right now and stop meeting with Peter. *Haven't a lot of men figured out how to be good fathers without all this? Is Peter going to tell me I'm wrong about everything?* Yet, Peter had not been telling him he was wrong about everything. He was talking to him straight, and he was treating Brian like a man. Besides, Brian had no clue how to navigate the pattern of every-other-weekend visitation with his children. If Peter could help, it was worth it. He said, "Okay," but what he meant was, *I'm ready to be rebuilt. Please continue.*

"When people talk about men fulfilling a kingly role at home, people immediately assume the man will become a tyrant, someone who uses his position to indulge his every whim. But a biblical king is one who has the authority to serve his subjects. Yes, he rules, but his ruling is in obedience to God, and for the benefit of those he rules. In other words, as fathers, our leadership should be a blessing to our families, not a source of heartache for them. We are not to rule to please ourselves and for our own happiness. We rule to please God and for the welfare of our families. We rule to serve rather than to be served. When we get that, I mean *really* get it, when it settles from here" (Peter pointed at his head) "down to here" (he pointed at his heart) "then things begin to change. Our families should not fear us; they should find strength in our strength; emotional security in our own emotional security that we live out in our homes. That's biblical kingship. That is how God is our king, and it's how we are to reflect God's kingship in our homes."

Peter paused to let Brian process this before moving on. "Adam's kingly role is not the only detail that the original audience would have picked up on. When God commanded Adam to cultivate the Garden, the word *cultivate* means more than just to provide food. It also means to nurture it, to bring out its fullest potential. When God created the Garden, He created it with enormous potential. God's command to cultivate the Garden is a command to nurture it, to bring out that full potential and to make the Garden the best it could possibly be. This involves putting a deliberate stamp on the organization of the Garden, to impose both design and order on the Garden. It is a call to make it both beautiful to the eye, yet efficient for producing food for Adam and his family. It is a call to discover not just what is currently in the Garden, but also all the potential that God put there. And that potential is to be brought out to bless people. The call to cultivate is a call to human vocation, to work with what God has provided for the benefit of others. It is the command to work, to create, to build, to grow, to discover, and to do all this in service to others. It is a call to what today we call a job or a career."

"Wow, that's a whole lot packed into a single word."

"The first few chapters of Genesis pack a wallop into a very few words. It is meant to be read slowly and to be pondered over a long period of time. I am summarizing this for you, but I hope you will spend some time in the next couple weeks rereading these verses and considering their full implications."

"I certainly will."

"Good. Now, for the original audience, the command to cultivate the Garden begins to image another role, that of the priest. For the original audience, a priest had two major functions to perform. First, he was responsible for nurturing and building up what was under his care. This meant nurturing and caring for both people and physical items, such as the plants of the Garden and the creatures of the earth. It would also apply to the things used in worship—remember that the Garden was the place to meet God, so it was a place of worship, not just Adam and Eve's home. Fulfilling this priestly role meant that Adam was supposed to ensure that the things under his responsibility were taken care of and used properly. By the same token, he was also responsible for nurturing the people in his care, encouraging them, and building them up. For the things in his care, it meant improving them, bringing out the full potential of what he has been given, both the potential of the earth and the plants of the Garden. Toward Eve, it meant encouraging her growth and building her up in her relationship with God. The priestly role was more than a call to service in the Garden itself; it was a call to service toward the people in the Garden."

"You mean Eve," Brian said.

"Yes, Eve, but also whatever children Adam and Eve may have. Remember, at this point, the Fall has not happened, so there is still the expectation that Adam and Eve will have children and continue to live in the Garden. Motherhood and fatherhood were baked into the original plan for women and men."

Brian was confused. "The way you make this nurturing stuff sound, it feels more like you're describing a mother than a father. Aren't mothers more nurturing than fathers?"

"We're looking at the way things are supposed to be, not the way they are after the Fall. We need to understand what was intended in the first place before we can understand where we are now and where we need to get to as men and fathers. Now, that said, are you surprised that fathers are supposed to be nurturing and encouraging?"

"I am, yeah. I think of moms as the ones who nurture and encourage and fathers as the disciplinarians."

"Mmm-mmm-mmm, you sexist pig," Peter said with a smile. They laughed. "I agree with you that *on balance,* moms tend to be the nurturing ones and dads the disciplinarians. However, some moms are excellent disciplinarians, and some fathers are outstanding at nurturing. Everyone has their strengths and weaknesses as parents. Although there are tendencies we can point to when we look at large numbers of parents, at the individual level, those tendencies may not mean much."

"True enough."

"Now, earlier I said that a priest had two major functions. The first role is to nurture and to care. The second role is that he represents. Depending on the moment, he either represents people to God, or he represents God to people. And we see this in the Garden too."

"Where?"

"Adam was created first and given instructions. These are instructions that are given not just to Adam the individual, but to Adam as the representative of the entire human race. As we have been talking about God's instructions to Adam, we have understood them as applying to everyone, not just Adam. Why? Because Adam did indeed represent everyone before God. And there's more. Remember I said that his kingly role was meant to represent God's true kingship? This means representing God to humanity. Both sides of the representation are present: Adam represents all of humanity before God, and he is supposed to represent God to all the people who will come after him."

"So," Brian interrupted, "are you telling me that this representing thing applies to me too?"

"I am. Just as Adam was to represent God to those who were supposed to join him in the Garden, so we as husbands and fathers are supposed to represent God to our families. Who we are and how we live our lives at home is supposed to point our family to the true God. They are supposed to learn what God is like by first learning what we are like."

"Whoa, hang on," Brian said, holding up his hands defensively. "That's crazy. How are my kids supposed to learn about God from *me*? I mean, there's nothing special about me. I go to church, but I'm not particularly holy or anything. I'm not a priest or a pastor. I can barely navigate my way through the Bible. How am *I* supposed to represent God to my children?"

"Well, if the only way to represent God to your children was to be a pastor or a theologian, then, yes, you would be in trouble. But there is a saying that has a lot of truth in it that I want you to remember. The saying is this: *The most important lessons in life are not taught, they're caught.* For you as a father, the most important lessons you will teach your children are caught, not taught. They are caught by what your children observe about you as a man. What they observe about what it means to put God first in your life, about the importance of daily prayer, about how you face the difficult issues in your life as one who seeks to honor God above all. You don't have to be perfect in all these things; your family can still see God in you even when you fail, if your heart was genuinely focused on pleasing God and blessing your family. God can use your mistakes just as well as he can use your successes. Don't think you need to have formal classroom instruction to represent God to your family—far from it! People need to *see* God in your life before they will listen to you talk about God. If they don't see God in your life, then they won't listen to what you have to say about God.

"Unfortunately, too many Christians attempt to lecture their children about God while remaining oblivious to how their lives at home undermine what they say. If your words and actions don't line up, your family will know you are a hypocrite. If, however, you try and fail, but your try matches your words, your children will understand. In fact, the vulnerability to try and fail is an important part of your kingly duty to create an emotionally safe home, one where it's okay to attempt things and fail at them. You don't need to be perfect, but you do need to be real."

Brian sighed. "In a strange way, although you're dumping a lot on my shoulders, it—I don't know—it doesn't feel like a heavy burden that I will collapse under. And yet this is a staggering load you're putting on me."

"That's good to hear. It means you're beginning to see that being a father is something you were created to do. On the one hand, it is an awesome and heavy responsibility that no one could ever possibly live up to. On the other hand, it's something that feels doable. That's the paradox of fatherhood. It's totally doable, and yet it's totally not. You were created for this, and yet there is no way you can live up to it. Yes, you can master this, but only by the grace of God."

"This is starting to sound a little Zen-like," Brian quipped.

"No, not Zen," Peter replied. "But it's important that you recognize you were created for this, and yet you cannot do it on your own. You need God to strengthen you to do it right. And in case you still think you can do this on your own, remember I have only covered two of the three roles we find in Adam."

Brian sighed. "Of course, there is another role. We wouldn't want to make this too easy."

"Exactly. Now, we've discussed the kingly role and the priestly role. There's one more, and that's the prophetic role. A prophet had two functions: to declare the will of the Lord and to call people to repentance. However, since this is before the Fall, there is nothing to repent from so, for Adam, the prophetic role only involved declaring the will of the Lord."

"Wait. I thought prophets also foretold the future."

"Foretelling the future was how a prophet validated his message,[8] but his true function was to declare the will of the Lord. All the prophets in the Old Testament and the New simply declared the will of God, whether it was God's will for the present time or the future. Their job was to receive that message from God and to make it known."

"Okay, so where do we see that with Adam?" Brian asked.

"Remember, I said to pay attention to the order of things. In Genesis 2:15, God gives Adam two commands; then, in the next two verses, he restricts him from eating the fruit of a single tree. After that, Adam names the animals and then God creates Eve at the end of chapter 2. At the start of chapter 3, the serpent tempts Eve. And notice verses 2 and 3." Peter pointed to his Bible as they read the verses.

> 2 And the woman said to the serpent, "From the fruit of the trees of the garden we may eat;
>
> 3 but from the fruit of the tree which is in the middle of the garden, God has said, 'You shall not eat from it or touch it, or you will die.'"

"Eve is quoting from the command God gave to Adam. My question for you, Brian, is this: From whom did Eve learn about that command?"

"From God. Just as God told the command to Adam, he told Eve too. Look, she says 'God has said.' God told her."

"I don't think so. Compare what she says in 3:3 to what God said in 2:17. Tell me what is different between them."

2:17 "but from the tree of the knowledge of good and evil
you shall not eat, for in the day that you eat from it you shall
surely die."

3:3 "but from the fruit of the tree which is in the middle of
the garden, God has said, 'You shall not eat from it or touch
it, lest you die.'"

Brian read them carefully and then suddenly looked up. "God
never said they couldn't touch the tree, only that they're not supposed
to eat from it."

"Very good. So, given that she screwed it up, do you suppose it was
God who taught her this command?" Peter asked.

Brian pursed his lips. "Yeah, I see your point. It's highly unlikely. So,
that means she would have learned about it from Adam. Are you saying
that Adam screwed it up and added something to God's command?"

"Let's leave how the addition to God's command came about until
next time we meet. Instead, I want to focus on the fact that Adam
taught Eve the instructions that he received from God. When we read
this story through the eyes of the original audience, we see Adam
exercising the prophetic role; he declared the will of the Lord to Eve."

"Well, okay," Brian said, "but it looks like he didn't do a very good
job teaching her."

"He didn't," Peter answered, "but we'll get to that the next time
we meet. For now, I want you to step back and see the three roles that
Adam fulfilled. What are they?"

"The kingly role, the priestly role, and the prophetic role."

"Excellent! Very good. And remember that the Garden was more
than just a garden; it was Adam and Eve's home. So, let's put all this
together. God created Adam to fulfill the roles of prophet, priest, and
king in his home. Ultimately, he was to fulfill those roles for the entire
human race but, for now, we want to see how this applies to

fatherhood. As a husband and as a father, Adam was to fulfill the duties of a prophet, priest, and king at home. Do you see it?"

"Um . . . yeah, I do. Wow. There's a lot going on in chapter 2. But . . . okay. So what? What does all this mean to me as a father?"

"That's a great question. When we talk about Adam, we are normally looking at him as the first human, the representative of all humans. However, now we're looking at him for what he tells us about God's design for fatherhood. We can look at fatherhood through the lens of the roles God gave to Adam, the roles of prophet, priest, and king.

"For example, the role of the king is to provide and protect. So, as fathers, we need to look at what we are providing. Are we providing for the material needs of our children? We don't need to give our children everything they want, but we should do everything we can to provide what they need. Moreover, are we providing for the emotional needs of our children? Do our children feel comfortable with us, or would they prefer to stay away from us? Do they feel safe with us, or are they afraid of us? Are they relaxed around us, or are they tense?

"Consider the priestly role. The role of the priest is to nurture and represent. How are we nurturing our children? Do we encourage them? Do we give them the emotional strength and confidence they need? Do we challenge them appropriately to achieve? Do they feel comfortable talking to us? And in terms of representing, this goes two ways. First, how do we represent our children before the Lord? We pray for them. We pray for them regularly and sincerely. We make praying for our children a priority. Second, how do we represent God to our children? We ditch the hypocrisy and selfishness and make the decision to live for the Lord. Moreover, we let our children in on our struggle to follow the Lord. We pray *with* them. We take them to church. We get involved with them spiritually . . . well, in an age-appropriate way. You won't have deep discussions about God with your three-year-old, but you get the idea.

"And finally, there is the prophetic role. We ensure our children are learning the Bible and how to apply it to their lives. Also, whatever church practices you follow, whether you have a liturgical calendar and liturgical practices or not, your church will still have activities you do as a church family that your children will need to know how to navigate. Teaching them how to live like a Christian is fulfilling your prophetic role with your children. It is also teaching them with your life. It is living your own life under God's authority and giving your children a living example of what that looks like.

"So, Brian, putting the three roles all together, we get a lens by which we can view what we are supposed to be doing as fathers. It gives us the viewpoint to both evaluate where we are, and it provides a road map for how we are to conduct ourselves as fathers."

"Okay, I see it. But . . . I don't know."

"What's bothering you?"

"What's bothering me is that I get my kids every other weekend for about forty-seven hours. How does this apply to me given how little time I have with them? I mean, this would have been really helpful before me and Bethany split up. But now it looks like . . ." Brian's voice trailed off.

"It looks like a complete waste of time?" Peter finished helpfully.

"Yes, exactly. A waste of time."

"Yeah, I thought the same thing, too, when I was in your shoes. But when I dove into the three roles, I realized that although the roles were damaged by divorce, they were still present. For example, in the kingly role, you are required to provide materially for your kids through child support. And you probably have a government agency keeping track of those records, right?"

"Yeah. Those guys make the mafia look like a cuddly teddy bear."

Peter laughed. "I remember. Those guys are awful. They have a crummy job to do. Just remember that they will keep the child support records straight. They're awful to try to talk to but, in the long term, they are a good deal. So, in terms of providing material support, you don't have an option; you're forced to do it. But now look at the emotional support you can give. The internet provides numerous ways to stay in touch with your children. And look at how you spend your time together as opportunities to be encouraging and supportive. As for providing protection, that functionality is damaged. If you don't live with your children, it's tough to provide unless you happen to live close to them. But even then, their mother probably doesn't want you hanging around. But just because your kingly role is damaged doesn't mean it's gone. Make the most of your kingly role when you have them, and look for reasonable opportunities beyond that.

"As for the priestly role, you can always pray for your children. Never underestimate the importance of a father praying regularly and faithfully for his children. Additionally, you can nurture your children when you spend time with them, both virtually on the internet or in person. And you can always walk the walk as a Christian. Your kids will see it.

"As for your prophetic role, you will have to do that as opportunity permits. To be honest, I found this the most challenging role as a divorced dad. It was difficult to teach my children the Bible every other weekend when in the intervening twelve days they got nothing. If Bethany is on board—"

Brian interrupted. "She's not."

"Okay. But even though this role is more challenging, it's not impossible. Look for opportunities to teach your children the Bible and show them how to apply its lessons. It will need to be age-appropriate, of course, but it can still be done."

After a few moments of looking away and thinking, Brian said, "Wow, there is so much here. It feels overwhelming."

"It can feel overwhelming at first. But use the three roles to keep focused on what you need to do as a father. It's difficult at the beginning because you're not used to it. But stick with it, ask God for strength and guidance to live into those roles, and it will make more sense as you continue. Now, before we go, I want to leave you with a little homework for the next time we meet." Brian groaned and rolled his eyes. "Now, now, Brian," Peter said with one of his crooked smiles. "Anything worth doing takes effort. Now, there are three things I want you to do. The first is to analyze how you are currently performing in your roles as prophet, priest, and king. What are you doing well, and what needs improvement? Be honest without beating yourself up too much. Remember, this is just where you are now, not where you will always be.

"The second thing I want you to do is to go back and revise your answers to the questions I asked you last time. But this time, I want you to take your roles as prophet, priest, and king into account. What do you want your children to say about you at your funeral? And how will you live your life so that your children will eulogize you without having to lie?

"The third thing I want you to do is the most important; keep planning and journaling. I want you to continue planning how you will spend your time with your kiddos and how you can reach out to them even when you can't be physically present over the next two weeks. I want you to look for opportunities to live out your three roles. Be deliberate, but don't be over-the-top about it. Look for opportunities to be a prophet, priest, and king to your kiddos. Okay, do you have all that?"

Brian listed the tasks to ensure he understood. "First, analyze my current performance. Second, revise my answers to the previous two questions considering my roles as prophet, priest, and king. Finally, look for opportunities to live those roles out with my children between now and the next time we meet."

"You've got it!" Peter checked his watch. "I'm late, I need to go. I look forward to seeing you in two weeks. I'm especially interested to hear how it goes with your kiddos. Goodbye."

"Goodbye." Brian watched Peter leave. He pulled out his phone and began furiously typing notes. His mind was racing with ideas.

Summary of Key Points

- We must read the Bible as the original audience would have read it, not how twenty-first-century people read it now. Otherwise, we will make the text say things the author never intended.

- Like a good father, God showed Adam his own need for Eve rather than just springing her on him.

- Fulfilling a kingly role in the home means you live sacrificially for your subjects and will lay down your life to protect them. It means that you do what it takes to ensure they are provided for rather than that you are provided for. Finally, it means you sacrifice your personal wishes to provide an emotionally healthy home.

- God calls men to live for something more than themselves and even more than their families; he calls them to live for God.

- We are not to rule to please ourselves or for our own happiness. We rule to please God and for the welfare of our families. We rule to serve rather than to be served.

- Our families should not fear us; they should find strength in our strength and emotional security in our emotional security that we live out in our homes.

- The most important lessons in life are not taught, they're caught. As a father, the most important lessons you will teach your children are what they observe about you as a man.

• You were created to be a father. On the one hand, it is an awesome and heavy responsibility that no one could ever possibly live up to. On the other hand, it feels totally doable. That's the paradox of fatherhood. It's totally doable, and yet it's totally not. You can master it, but only by the grace of God.

• The prophetic role is to declare the will of God to his family. This is done by teaching his family about God and living his life as a demonstration of what it means to live under God's authority.

• The priestly role is to nurture and represent. We nurture our children by giving them emotional strength, confidence, and appropriate challenges. We represent our children before God by praying regularly for them. We represent God to our children by living transparently for the Lord.

4 Temptation, Deception, and Scheming

Genesis 3

Two weeks later, Brian turned sharply into the restaurant parking lot. He was late . . . again. The kids gave their father hugs, but this time they were not forced. They had enjoyed their weekend with Brian, and it showed both in their smiles and in the conversation for most of the drive to meet Bethany. As they buckled them into her minivan, Bethany muttered that she wondered why she even bothers being on time. He didn't take the bait. He knew she was jealous that the kids had enjoyed their weekend. Brian suppressed his smile. He said his goodbyes, closed the car door and waved as they drove off.

He found Peter waiting for him inside. They ordered, sat down, and Brian watched as Peter globbed up his French fries with ketchup and consumed the first one. Peter sighed deeply with a smile on his face.

Brian waited for it. And he waited some more. But it didn't come. He motioned to Peter.

"What?" asked Peter.

"I'm waiting for 'Lord, have mercy on me, a sinner.'"

Peter smiled, then looked around quickly in a mock conspiratorial way. "I have to confess, I had some fries two days ago, so these are not as special as when I go two weeks between orders."

"Except that 'Lord, have mercy on me, a sinner' is like an opening prayer or something. Our meeting feels incomplete without it. I feel like if we start without it, God will zap us or something."

Peter laughed. "No, He's not going to zap us, but I'll keep the opening prayer in mind for next time. I want to know how your weekend went. But first tell me how you adjusted your answers in light of your roles as prophet, priest, and king."

Brian perked up. "Well, two things jumped out at me. The first was my kingly role. I have been trying to keep the same rules for my children as Bethany has at her house. I thought it would make it easier on the kids. However, they don't work as well at my place. Where I live is more cramped than what they have at Bethany's: we have to share a bathroom, the living room is smaller . . . well, you get the idea. So, I decided that part of my role as king is that I can change the rules. When I got the kiddos back to my place, I told them, 'Mom's house, Mom's rules; Dad's house, Dad's rules.' And then I explained to them what needed to change."

"How many things did you change?"

"Three things and they involved what I call the nighttime routine, how they get ready to go to bed. Then on both Friday and Saturday nights, I reminded them of the new routine. They took right to it. I thought changing the rules and routines would be difficult, but it was pretty easy."

"Wow," Peter exclaimed, "that's fantastic! I love that you told them 'Mom's house, Mom's rules; Dad's house, Dad's rules.' That does so many things at once. First, it elevates you from being a mere babysitter to being their father. Second, it establishes rules. Kids need rules to follow. Proper boundaries give them a sense of safety. Third, you did not overwhelm them with a whole bunch of new rules at once. Fourth, you reminded them of the rules. And, finally, you did it all in a loving way. That's really outstanding—good for you!"

Brian nearly blushed at the praise. "Thank you. The other thing I did was to recognize I am not very good in my priestly role. I'm not very good at praying for Megan and Brian Jr. So, I bought a book of prayers on the internet. It has some prayers for children. I've been using that to pray for my children. And I think it helped. This weekend, I was calmer with them. I didn't get upset with them when they did dumb things. In fact, I kind of laughed at the absurdity of some of it."

Peter smiled like a proud father whose son had just kicked the winning field goal. "Fantastic! This is so great to hear."

Brian was encouraged. He continued, "I also realized I'm not very good at encouraging my kids. So, to practice encouraging them, I borrowed the game Chutes & Ladders from a friend and played it with them. The game itself is dumb, but they enjoyed it. I think we played it ten times. Anyway, it gave me a chance to work on encouraging them and laughing with them and just . . . I don't know . . . enjoying the time with them. It was a very relaxed weekend. Well, it was relaxed until Brian Jr. tried to eat one of the pieces." Brian laughed at the memory. "But no harm no foul. I enjoyed this weekend more than I have any other so far. And . . . I don't know. I was just more patient with them this weekend."

"I could see that they enjoyed their weekend when they got out of your car," Peter said. "It was all over their faces. You took what you learned in Genesis and began adapting it to your situation. And better still, you didn't try to do everything all at once either. You bit off a few small opportunities and went with them. You did well, Brian. You did *very* well." Peter put his hand on Brian's shoulder. "I'm proud of you."

Brian looked down to hide his blushing. He had no idea that a commendation from Peter would mean so much to him, but it did. He nearly teared up. "Thank you," he said softly, afraid that if he spoke any louder his voice would crack.

Peter gave Brian a moment to pull himself together before continuing. "Now, tell me about your homework. How did you change your answers to the two questions?"

Brian answered, "Well, I've been thinking a lot about that, and my answer is that I don't want to share my answer yet. I mean, I adjusted my answers, but now they just sound hokey, like I'm filling in the blanks rather than giving an answer from my heart. I want more time with them. Please don't think I'm not working on them. I'm just not ready to share them yet."

"I understand. The fact that you've already been implementing what you've learned so far tells me how seriously you're taking this. Just know that my desire to hear your answers is not for my sake but for yours. Verbalizing your answers takes them from being vague intentions to something concrete. It will also give you an opportunity to refine them and get feedback to make sure they are realistic. But with that said, take your time. I know this is difficult."

"Thank you." Brian motioned to Peter's Bible. "I have a question. You taught me what the Bible says, but not specific steps on how to live it out. Every Bible study I've been a part of always has an application, something I can go do to live it out. Yet you haven't done that except journaling and a couple of questions to answer. Why? When you teach me what the Bible says, aren't you going to show me how to live it out?"

Peter grinned his crooked smile as if he had been half expecting this question. "I'd love to tell you how to live it out. The problem is that I can't."

"What?" Brian was incredulous. "If you can't tell me how to live it out, then why are you wasting my time?"

"Hang on, let me explain. What I am doing is giving you a deep dive into what the Bible says about fatherhood. We can talk about fatherhood at a high level, but the actual implementation of fatherhood is another matter. There are so many permutations of fatherhood that it is impossible to say, '*This* is how to live it out.' There is no one-size-fits-all, cookie-cutter approach to fatherhood Think about it. A residential father has a completely different situation from a nonresidential father. And even with residential fathers, family structures are very different. Imagine two different scenarios. The first father is, say, an HVAC technician. He leaves home at 6:00 a.m. to go to work. In the summer, he is outside under the blazing sun or crawling around stifling attics fixing air-conditioning. In the winter, he is outside in the cold fixing furnaces. He comes home having worked twelve hours. Imagine for a moment what his evening with the family is like. The next scenario is a software manager. He works from home full time. In the morning, he helps to get his kids off to school, then he shuffles into his home office about 8:00 a.m., works until the kids get home, gets them situated, then returns to work in his home office until about 6:00 p.m. Considering the situations of these two men, are they going to implement what the Bible says in anything close to the same way?"

Brian objected, "Well, their jobs are different, they may have different energy levels at night, but being a father is being a father, right?"

"Okay, so let's keep going with the scenarios. In the case of our HVAC technician, suppose his wife is a stay-at-home mom. How does that affect his fatherhood? Or suppose that she is a trial attorney who must often work late preparing for court. How would that affect his fatherhood? For our software manager, suppose his wife is an airline pilot who is often gone during the week. How would that affect his fatherhood?

"And let's also consider each man's hobbies. Let's say our HVAC father is a sports junkie. On the other hand, let's say our software manager father loves science fiction and superhero movies. How would these hobbies affect his fatherhood? How would it affect their fatherhood if their wives supported their hobbies? What if their spouses didn't support their hobbies?"

Peter continued relentlessly, "How would it affect their fatherhood if one or both have a special-needs child? What if one or both fathers have a parent who is seriously ill and needs his care? What if one or both are struggling with chronic illness themselves? What if one or both are recovering from a failed business venture that left him saddled with debt? What if one or both are dealing with a blended family, either with both of their kids from previous relationships living in the home or maybe Mom's kids live at home full time, while his kids visit every other weekend? And here's a killer: How would it affect their fatherhood if one or both have ever struck their children in a fit of anger . . . or worse? Or, to turn it around, what if the mother is the abusive one? What if the mother considers the children *her* children, and considers the father little better than an ATM machine and will not accept his input as to how the children are raised?"

Peter wasn't finished. "Now let's also consider nonresidential fathers. There's a big difference between every-other-weekend visits versus, say, every-other-weekend and Wednesdays, or a week with Mom and a week with Dad visitation schedule. The living situations of nonresidential fathers directly impact how fatherhood is lived out. And for all the talk of Mom and Dad getting along for the sake of the kids, in my experience, that is more talk than reality. How does it affect fatherhood if Mom is playing games or doesn't support visitation with the father? What if what she says is accurate, and she split with him to protect her children? Alternately, what about situations where the mother is insanely jealous of the father? What if the custodial mother always trash-talks him to the children?

"Consider fathers who were never married to the mother of their children, or fathers who have been absent from the lives of their children for a long time and are attempting to reestablish relationships with them. How do long absences affect fatherhood? What about men who walked out on their families and are now seeking to make amends with their children? What about men who were gone because they served prison terms?

"And finally, just to pile on, what about cultural differences? How fatherhood is lived out in Massachusetts is different from how it's done in Montana. And what about location in terms of living in a rural place or suburbia, or downtown in the heart of a large city? How does location in America affect fatherhood? And what about the differences between entirely different cultures, say Mongolia and Morocco? Each is a culturally distinct place that will put its own spin on fatherhood.

"The reality, Brian, is that people tend to either universalize or trivialize our own experiences. Some folks think that their situation is the situation nearly everyone faces. It's not. While for others, they think that their situation is utterly unique, and no one has ever faced it before. That's not true either. But when we talk about fatherhood, we have to be careful to realize that there are many, *many* permutations of fatherhood. That is why I prefer to stick with what the Bible says, and then give you tools so you can figure out how to apply it in your unique circumstances. If I attempt to tell you how to apply it, chances are I will merely read my situation or my view of American fatherhood into your state of affairs. Most of the books on fatherhood I've read do exactly that. They espouse a view of fatherhood that is really a white-collar, upper middle-class perspective based on American suburbia. That's really great if you happen to be a white-collar, middle class residential father in suburbia, but how applicable is it for a nonresidential father living in a rough neighborhood in the heart of a city? Would it also be applicable, say, to a cab driver in Manila? Probably not.

"My plan is to show you what the Bible teaches about fatherhood and give you tools so you can apply it to your circumstances. But I'm not going to tell you a lot of specifics about how you should be living out fatherhood; that is up to you to seek God and determine His will for how he wants you to be a father to your children. It is highly unlikely that God wants you to live out your fatherhood as He wanted me to live mine out. Yes, there are general principles God wants us to know. But how we live them out will be very different. This is why I gave you the first two questions; they are meant to help you start with the end in mind. Having the end in mind is always a good place to begin planning. Those questions will guide you as you translate God's general principles into your unique circumstance. I would love to give you a cookie-cutter approach to fatherhood, but it would be a lie. There is no one-size-fits-all approach to fatherhood."

Brian needed a moment to process that. "Wow. I guess I never considered all the different ways men live out fatherhood."

"Most men are so overwhelmed with their own situation that that don't have the time to consider all the permutations of fatherhood. So, my plan is to teach you what the Bible says, and then I'll coach you through how you apply it to your circumstance. Does that sound fair to you?"

"It does. So, what do you have for me today?"

Peter opened his Bible and placed it on the table so they could both see it. "The last time we met we looked at the three roles of the man, and we saw how it applied to fatherhood. I also said we would cover what happened to Adam and Eve in the Garden. This is important because we can talk about the ideals of fatherhood, but we don't live in an ideal world. We need to comprehend how it all went wrong to understand what we face as fathers today."

Brian interrupted. "But I know this story. Eve ate the forbidden fruit, and then God kicked them out of the Garden."

"Well, yes, but there's more to it than that. Remember that the first few chapters of Genesis packs a lot into a few words. I want us to consider just how big a wallop it delivers. Now, remember the setup. God created Adam, gave him the command to cultivate and keep the Garden, and then created the woman to be his suitable companion, someone who will live out God's commands with him. Remember, also, I've been stressing the importance of reading Genesis through the eyes of the original audience, and Genesis 3 is no exception. We need to understand the Garden through their eyes.

"In those days, kings had gardens. A king's garden did two things. First, it provided the food the king would eat. On the one hand, it was a place to grow a wide variety of foods. Kings are going to have the best. Also, kings were always concerned about being poisoned, so they controlled their food from ground to plate. A king's garden was the place where the food he would eat was grown, and the safety of the food could be managed. The second thing a garden did was to give a king a place to go to unwind after a hard day, to decompress. Not just anyone could enter a king's garden; that was a protected place. The king's garden was his sanctuary. Also, it's unlikely the king himself did any actual gardening; he would hire that out. Now, seeing what a king's garden was supposed to be, what does it tell you that God placed Adam in the Garden to cultivate it and keep it?"

Brian spoke slowly, not entirely sure his answer was correct. "Well, it was a position of privilege. If Adam was responsible for growing the king's food, then that was a special position. It required skill to maintain the king's garden. This wasn't a cushy job, but it was a job with real responsibilities. The king put a lot of trust in the person who grew his food."

"Very good," Peter said, encouragingly. "Keep going."

"And if the king went to his garden to relax and unwind, then the gardener would have to leave him alone, to let him be so the king can decompress. He would have to know how to do his job while working around the king's schedule."

"Um, think a little more carefully. Let me give you a hint. You're imagining the gardener as a menial servant. However, if access to the king's garden was restricted yet the gardener got to be alone with the king, what does that say about the relationship between the gardener and the king?"

Brian thought about it. "Well, it would mean that the king would have to trust the gardener. I mean, he would have to *really* trust the gardener."

"Good. But there would be several servants who would have one-on-one time with the king. What does it say that the gardener got one-on-one time when the king was done doing business, when he just needed to relax?"

"Well . . . it means that . . ." Brian's voice trailed off in thought until it came to him. "It means that the gardener would have been a trusted servant. He would have known the king when the king was letting his hair down, so to speak. The gardener was not just a gardener but someone the king could relax with. We are closest to the people we relax with. The gardener would have been close to the king, a friend. Maybe even a best friend."

"Exactly! Now, let's apply that to Adam. What does it tell us about the relationship God expected to have with Adam when he put him in the Garden?"

"Well, it tells us that . . . *wow*! It tells us that God expected to be very close friends with Adam, maybe even best friends. God wanted a relationship where they could just be real with each other, where they could just talk and hang out. They could just be friends together. Wow!"

"Yeah, wow," Peter agreed.

"This is strange because I always thought God was distant and unapproachable. I thought we were supposed to use 'thee' and 'thou' when we pray to Him, really formal language. Something like, 'O, Lordeth, we cometh before thee today to beseech thee in thy beaditudinest mercies' or something like that."

Peter laughed. "'Beaditudinest mercies.' That's funny! But you bring up a good question; how formal do we need to be in our prayers when we approach God? Some people are hyperformal in all their prayers, treating God just like you said: as a presence that's distant and unapproachable, uncaring and unloving. But what we see in the Garden is something completely different. On the other hand, some people go to the other extreme and start their prayers with a conversational 'Hey, God,' or something similar. I call this 'buddy-buddy' language, something you would say as a greeting to one of your buddies on the basketball court. I think buddy-buddy prayers are dangerous. When we pray, we can't lose sight of the fact that we are addressing the one who is both our king and our creator. Buddy-buddy language misses the position of the one we are addressing. A certain level of formality is correct. However, when God puts Adam in the Garden, He is demonstrating that he is not distant and unapproachable, nor is He cold and unloving. He may be our king and creator, but He desires to be friends with His people. He desires to be close friends, the one we go to when we need to talk things out, the one we confide in, and the one we go to when we just need to decompress after a tough day. What an incredible privilege!"

"When I pray, I normally just ask God for things; you know, prayer requests. But what you're saying is different. You're saying prayer can be as simple as unburdening myself to God."

"Yes, exactly. God wants you to be real with him. Look at the Book of Psalms. So many of David's psalms are David pouring out his frustration or anger or dismay over what was going on around him. Essentially, he didn't hesitate to ask, 'God, what the heck are you doing?' Yet, those same psalms are really an affirmation that David will follow God even when God isn't making any sense. David was called the man after God's own heart. He wasn't called that because he always did the right thing. David wasn't above making some boneheaded decisions. However, what set him apart was his desire to have that close relationship with God. He wasn't satisfied with a God who was distant; he sought God in the here and now. He desired a relationship with God that mirrored what Adam was supposed to have with God in the Garden. That's what made David's pursuit of God so special."

"And is that the same kind of relationship I am supposed to pursue with God?"

"Yes, it is. But think about what that closeness should look like. This is the relationship of an inferior to a superior, not the relationship of two equals. That doesn't mean it cannot be a close relationship, only that we as the inferior beings can never lose sight of the fact we are interacting with the God of the universe. That's why the buddy-buddy approach to prayer is so dangerous. It attempts to emphasize that God loves us and fully understands our struggles, but it does so at the expense of losing sight of His position as our king and creator."

Brian thought about Peter's words. "I feel like we've gotten off topic a little bit."

"A little bit, but let me bring us back with this. Think about what kind of relationship you should have with your children. You want to be close to your children, to be friends with them, right?" Brian nodded. "However, no matter what, you are still their father. You still maintain a position of authority over them. If they step out of line, you need to correct them or even discipline them. You are still the one who sets the rules, and you expect them to be obeyed. If you approach your relationship with your children trying to be their friend all the time, you will set your children up for a life of selfishness and unruly behavior because they did not have to obey their father's authority. You can never sacrifice your authority over them.

"By the same token, you want to be close to them. You want them to talk to you openly and honestly, to come to you with their problems, and to just hang out with you. This is the same kind of relationship God wants with us. He will not give up His authority, but He still desires to be close with us. As men and fathers, we are both fathers and children, we are both in authority and under authority. To put it another way, God makes us fathers so we can understand what His fatherhood over us looks like. We become fathers to our children so we can understand how to be better children of God the Father. Does that make sense?"

"Wow, yeah, it does. I never thought that having children was supposed to help me understand my relationship with God more. That's pretty mind-blowing."

"Now there's one more thing you need to understand about the Garden before we dive into what happened there. I said earlier that a king's garden was a protected place—not just anyone could enter the king's garden. Now if you were going to mark the boundaries of a garden, how would you do it?"

"I don't know. I guess I would build a wall around it."

"Good. But kings would be concerned that people would just crawl over the wall. So, they would add something to the wall; they would add images of the king. These might be little statues spaced out along the top of the wall. Now, let's see if you remember what you've learned so far. Why would putting images of himself on the wall stop people from scaling the wall?"

Brian thought about his answer. "Because in their day, the king's image stood for the king himself. What you did to the image you did to the man. So, when you crawled over the image, in a sense you crawled directly over the king."

"That's right, very good. The image of the king was the warning not to pass, or not to crawl over the wall. If someone did it anyway, they did it as if they directly and deliberately defied the king. Once he was caught, that person was going to experience a *very* bad day. Surrounding the king's garden with images of himself was a display of the king's strength.

"But let me ask you this, Brian. In Genesis 1 we read that Adam and Eve were created in the image of God. God did not use inanimate stone statues for his image like human kings did; he created living beings to represent him. And in Genesis 2 we saw that the man was given the command to keep the Garden, and we saw that *keep* was a military term. It meant to stand guard and protect the Garden from those who had no authority to be within it. In both the creation of humanity in the image of God and in the command to keep the Garden, man's function was to protect the Garden from those who would enter it to defile and despoil it. Do you see that?"

"Yeah, I sure do. Except," Brian hesitated, "the Bible never describes any of this. If it's not in the Bible, how can you be sure of it?"

"Because we're reading it through the eyes of the original audience and approaching the text with their assumptions. That's what archaeologists do; they uncover the ancient world so we can see the world through their eyes. When we see things through their eyes, we begin to see the assumptions the original audience would have had. Let me give you a current example. If today I wrote about someone driving a car and making a left turn, do I need to describe how a steering wheel works? No, of course not. Because in our world, I can safely assume you know what's involved in making a car turn. In the same manner, it was safe to assume that the reader would know that a king's garden had a wall with images of the king. It's just the way things were."

"Okay, I can see that."

"All right, good. Then let's get to the text of Genesis 3."

> 1 Now the serpent was more crafty than any beast of the field which the LORD God had made. And he said to the woman, "Indeed, has God said, 'You shall not eat from any tree of the garden'?"

Peter looked up from the Bible. "Okay, I want you to start looking for what is wrong in the text. Think about what we have talked about in terms of the image of God and, also, the roles of prophet, priest, and king. Tell me the first thing you see wrong here."

"Well, if they are images of God who are supposed to keep away those who did not have authority to be there, then why didn't they throw out the serpent?"

"Exactly. The very fact that this conversation is going on shows us that they are neglecting God's command to keep the Garden, to stand guard and to throw out those who are not authorized to be there. Had Adam and Eve simply done what God told them to do and tossed the serpent out, the Fall never would have happened. Now, let's notice the next problem. Tell me what's wrong with the question the serpent asks."

"He's misquoting God. God did not say you shall not eat from any tree of the Garden. He said you may freely eat from any tree except for the one," said Brian.

"So, let's think about what the serpent is trying to do when he twists what God said. The original audience would have been shocked that God let Adam and Eve eat from any plant in the Garden except one. That was the king's food, not food for the gardener. When God opens the whole Garden up to humans except for one tree, the original audience would have been stunned by God's generosity. They would not have thought God was stingy to withhold a single tree; they would have been blown away that humans got to eat the food of the king at all. Such a thing was unheard of in their day. God's generosity would have been abundantly clear to them. What the serpent is trying to do is to cast aspersions at God, but he does it in stages. First, he misquotes God. This is the easy part to see if they accurately remember God's instructions or not. If they don't remember God's instructions, then getting them to violate God's actual commands is straightforward enough."

Brian interrupted. "The last time we met, we saw that she did remember the instruction . . . sort of."

"That's right. Look at Eve's answer in light of the serpent misquoting God."

> 2.17 And the woman said to the serpent, "From the fruit of the trees of the garden we may eat;

> 3.3 but from the fruit of the tree which is in the middle of the garden, God has said, 'You shall not eat from it or touch it, or you will die.'"

Peter pointed at verse 2. "Notice that Eve corrects the obvious error; they are allowed to eat freely in the Garden. But in verse 3, she adds the phrase 'or touch it.' God never said that. As gardeners, of course, they needed to touch the tree to cultivate it. That was their job. So, why would she add this in?"

"Because Adam taught her incorrectly?" Brian asked, a little confused.

"Meh, that only kicks the same problem from Eve to Adam. Why would he, she, or they add this in?"

"I'm just guessing, but maybe they figured better safe than sorry?"

"Yes, that's exactly right. If eating the fruit of that tree would lead to death, it makes sense, then, to not even touch it. If doing something leads to death, then not only will I not do that thing, but I won't even go near it. This is called fencing the law of God. If God has said not to do something, people will put a fence around it with the idea that if we prohibit ourselves from even going near it, then we can never be guilty of performing the wrong behavior. For example, the second commandment warns against taking the name of God, *Yahweh*, in vain.[9] So, what did the Jews do? When they read the Scriptures aloud and came across the name of God, *Yahweh*, they pronounced *adonai* instead, which means Lord. That's a classic example of fencing the law. If we never pronounce the name of God, then we can never be guilty of taking the name of God in vain. The same thing goes with Christians who refuse to drink any alcohol. The New Testament tells us not to be drunk because that is dissipation,[10] so some Christians argue that we should not drink *any* alcohol. If we don't drink any alcohol, then we can never be guilty of being drunk. Adam and Eve are doing the same thing. Do you see it?"

"Yes. But fencing the law seems reasonable to me. I mean, if doing a certain thing leads to death or really bad consequences, then why not avoid it altogether?"

"Sometimes there is wisdom to fencing the law, so long as you fence it for yourself and no one else. The problem with it is that it puts words into the mouth of God. God never said to avoid pronouncing His name; He said don't use His name in vain. God never said we should not drink any alcohol; He said we are not to be drunk. In the case of Adam and Eve, God never said not to touch the fruit of the one tree; He only said not to eat from that tree. If you think prudence demands extra precautions concerning a particular sin, then by all means have at it. That's your decision. But don't say that's what God said. He didn't. And be careful about putting your extra precautions on anyone else. When we put words into God's mouth like this, we inadvertently portray Him as a cosmic killjoy, like He always wants to take the joy out of life. When we fence the law and claim God said so, we cast aspersions at God as if He is holding something good back from us. He's not. In the case of this one tree, He is holding back something that Adam and Eve were not ready for yet.

"In fact, Brian, that is exactly what the serpent seizes on. As soon as Eve confesses to fencing the law, he jumps on the underlying assumption that God is withholding something good from her. Look at verses 4 and 5."

> 4 The serpent said to the woman, "You surely shall not die!

> 5 For God knows that in the day you eat from it your eyes will be opened, and you will be like God, knowing good and evil."

"In verse 4, the serpent outright lies. But notice that he rationalizes the lie in verse 5. He says that eating from this one tree will open your eyes, and you will get to enjoy all the good things that God gets to enjoy. The underlying assumption here is that God has been holding something back from Adam and Eve, and it's something really good. God is stingy and mean-spirited. He doesn't want you to enjoy the same good life that He gets to experience. Over time, this same temptation will get played out with different nuances, but it's always the same basic approach. God is holding back the good life from you because He is either stingy, or He's mean-spirited, or He just doesn't understand your situation, or He just doesn't care or . . . well, you can pick the reason of the day. The basic idea is that God is withholding something good from you.

"The reason I'm parking on this idea is that as a father, Brian, you will be tempted in the same manner as Eve. The specifics will be different, but the pattern will be the same. You'll get the idea that God is holding back the good life from you. If you'll only do this thing that God told you not to do, you'll be happier or wiser or wealthier or whatever it is that you think you're missing from obtaining the good life. Or another play on it is that God is holding back the good life from your children. As a parent that is potent stuff. No one wants to be a bad parent, and parents want their children to have a good life."

"I hear you, but can you give me an example?" Brian asked. "Can you show me what this looks like in the real world?"

"Sure. Let me give you an example that may feel a little trivial, but it shows the temptation in a real-world situation. Let's say you've had a really bad week at work. You get to Friday, and you're whipped, but this is your weekend for visitation, or you said you would do something special like attend your child's soccer game. You pick up your kiddos, take them home, and you're trying to get them ready for bed. They need to brush their teeth. Your oldest refuses. She says she brushed them before coming over. However, the rule you have in place is that they brush their teeth every night before going to bed. You have two temptations here, one involving you and the other involving your child. The one involving you is that it would be easier to give in. You're tired and emotionally wrung out after the week. You just want the kids in bed so you can relax for a few minutes and then go to bed yourself. Enforcing the rule is a hassle and you don't want to deal with upset children, especially if your relationship with them is tentative to begin with. Installing disciplined habits into your children is hard work, and children often resent it in the moment.[11] The 'good life' is doing what it takes to get the kids in bed so you can relax. On the other hand, the temptation directed at your children is that if they push back on the rules, they get to live the good life of doing whatever they want whenever they want. As a parent, I don't need to tell you how disastrous that is. In each case, the temptation is that life would be better if you don't do what God has instructed you to do. Does that help?"

"It does, thank you."

"Okay, then let's keep going with the text. Look at verse 6."

6 When the woman saw that the tree was good for food,
and that it was a delight to the eyes, and that the tree was
desirable to make one wise, she took from its fruit and ate;
and she gave also to her husband with her, and he ate.

"There are three things going on here, and all three are very important. First, notice the progression: it was good for food, a delight to the eyes, and desirable to make one wise. Eve looks at the fruit and rationalizes her sin by thinking that the fruit of the tree was good for food. It's nutritious. It's good for her. When she disobeyed, her mind fell. And the fruit was a delight to the eyes. That's another way of saying it was pretty. It looked good. This is a reference to her emotions. Just as her mind fell, so, too, did her emotions. Finally, the fruit was desirable to make one wise. *Desirable* is a reference to Eve's will. She desired the fruit—she wanted it. The point is that this was not a part of Eve that fell into sin; it was the totality of Eve. Her mind, her emotions, and her will were all involved. This was a deliberate, reasoned thing she did."

"So, Eve really screwed up, didn't she?"

"Yes, and it gets worse for Eve. However, wait until we get to Adam; that's when the situation becomes truly terrible. But let's finish with Eve. The second thing I want you to notice is where the Bible says, 'she took from its fruit and ate.' That does not mean she went over to the tree to eat from it, as if the temptation took place in another part of the Garden and then she walked over to the tree. No, she was standing there the entire time. Here's where I want you to think carefully for a moment. Eve has fenced the law by saying that they were not even supposed to touch the tree. My question is this: if she is not even supposed to touch the tree, then why is she standing either under it or minimally right next to it, having a conversation that she's not even supposed to be having? Why is she standing there of all places?"

Brian considered his answer. "Is it because she was already thinking about eating from the tree?"

"Yes, good. She was already thinking about it. But she can be thinking about it from any place within the Garden. Why is she standing right there at this moment?"

The question hung in the air until Brian finally pieced it together in his head. "Oh, it's because she *wanted* to be tempted. She *wanted* some sort of justification to eat from the tree."

"Yes, that's exactly right. Eve *wanted* to be tempted. This is so important to understand what happened in the Garden. A person can't be tempted with something he doesn't want. For example, no one could tempt me to do something by promising a plate full of Brussels sprouts covered in vinegar. I think that's disgusting, and I have no desire for them whatsoever. However, tempt me with a bucket of fries that won't clog my arteries, and you have my undivided attention."

"What about air-fried fries?" Brian asked mischievously.

"Yeah, we've covered that. Nice try. The point is that temptation is only successful when you are tempted with something you genuinely *want* to be tempted with. If you don't want it, the temptation fails. Eve wants to be tempted; that's why she's standing by the tree. And oh, by the way, she's standing there holding a conversation with the serpent who should have been thrown out. She is neither cultivating nor keeping the Garden. This is a total fail on her part."

"Yeah, she really blew it. And she blew it intentionally."

"Let's be careful how far we take the intentional part. 1 Timothy 2:14 makes it clear that Eve was deceived." Peter turned to 1 Timothy and laid out his Bible so they could both read it.

14 And it was not Adam who was deceived, but the woman being quite deceived, fell into transgression.

Peter said, "Eve was deceived; she was a dingbat. Now, granted, when you take daily walks with God in the Garden,[12] you have absolutely no excuse to be deceived. All Eve needed to do was to say something like, 'Hey, this sounds great. I just want to run it by God this afternoon when I see Him and make sure it's good to go.' But she didn't. Why? Because she was deceived.

"Now, Brian, pay close attention. This third thing I want you to see is where it gets really hard. 1 Timothy 2:14 tells us that Eve was deceived. My question is this: Was Adam equally deceived?"

"Well, yeah, sure," Brian answered.

Peter motioned to his Bible. "Look closer at the text."

Brian reread 1 Timothy 2:14. "Oh, no he wasn't deceived." He considered what it meant, and his eyes grew wide. "Oh, wow! Adam *wasn't* deceived. He knew what was going on the whole time."

"Yes, exactly. Adam was not deceived. Let's go back to Genesis 3:6." Peter flipped the pages of his Bible. "Notice that she gave to her husband who was with her. That means Adam was not somewhere else in the Garden when this exchange between Eve and the serpent went down. It means he was standing there the whole time, watching it happen. So, keep thinking carefully, Brian. If Adam was standing there the entire time and he was not deceived, then what was going on with Adam? What was he thinking? What did he want?"

"Well, I guess he also wanted to eat the fruit from the tree."

"Yes. Keep going."

"But he was concerned that the fruit would be deadly to him," Brian said, continuing to draw out the implications.

"And so . . . ?" Peter asked, encouraging Brian to continue.

"And so . . . and so . . ." Brian said, unsure of where this was going until suddenly, he saw it. He inhaled reflexively and his eyes grew wide. "Oh, what a jerk! He totally threw Eve under the bus to get what he wanted. He figured if she ate it and lived, he would have some too. But if she ate it and died, then better her than him. Oh, wow! Son of a—" Brian stopped from finishing his thought aloud as he saw children eating nearby.

"You got it," Peter said. "You're completely right; Adam threw Eve under the bus. He was willing to put her in mortal danger to get what he wanted. If she died, well, too bad, so sad. His complete indifference to Eve is chilling. A lot of people want to put all the blame on Eve for the Fall, but that's misplaced. The truly consequential sin was Adam's. In fact, the Bible never refers to this as the sin of Eve or even the sin of Adam *and* Eve. It refers to it as the sin of Adam.[13] Consider the ways Adam failed. First, he failed in his kingly role when he failed to throw the serpent out of the Garden and failed to protect Eve. That was the command to keep the Garden. Second, he failed in his priestly role when he put his own selfishness above Eve's good. All Adam needed to do was encourage Eve not to eat the fruit until they talked it over with God first. And finally, he failed in his prophetic role both when he fenced the law, and when he failed to apply God's command to the specific situation. God said don't eat from the tree, and there were no exceptions given. The application was straightforward, but Adam failed to carry it out. He failed in his prophetic role, he failed in his priestly role, and he failed in his kingly role. And unlike Eve, Adam was not deceived about any of it."

"It was a total fail."

"Yeah, it was a total fail. Now let's bring this around to how it applies to fatherhood. When Adam fell, his very nature changed. He was created in a state of innocence where he could choose not to sin. But because of his actions here, his state transformed. Sin would now taint his entire life and everything he did. Worse, his sinfulness was passed on to the entire human race[14] so that everything we do is tainted by sin. As fathers, we are constantly tempted to sin in the same way as Adam. We are tempted to throw our wives and our families under the bus, so to speak; we sacrifice them to get what we want. Men will sacrifice their wives for their careers, for their hobbies, and for their addictions. Let me be clear that this is more than spending too much time at work. Men are just as ambitious about whatever sports team or social media or personal interest they may have. Whatever it is that men want, or wherever they get affirmation, they will pursue that while their wives and families are left to pay the price for that ambition."

"Are you saying all men do this?" Brian asked.

"No. I'm not saying that all men sin like Adam and all women sin like Eve. I think Adam and Eve represent the two major ways people rebel against God. Either we are selfish, conniving, and deliberate like Adam, or we're foolishly deceived dingbats like Eve. In my experience, I've seen my share of dingbat dudes and selfish, conniving women. As fathers, however, we need to be very aware of the tendency to abuse the roles God has given to us. We need to be aware when we are throwing our wives and children under the bus so we can get what we want. Remember, a king is supposed to serve his people, not use them to get what he wants.

"You're still a young man, Brian. You need to be aware that you will be constantly tempted to abuse your God-given roles as prophet, priest, and king. The last time we met, I told you what the original design was. Now we must confront the reality we live in. Your kingly role will always be under assault. That assault will come in two different directions. The first is that you risk abusing your kingly role by becoming a tyrant in your home. You will be tempted to throw your authority around like you have ultimate power and there is no one to stop you. This is the temptation to be abusive and manipulative. The second direction that temptation will come is for you to abdicate your kingly role entirely. You will be tempted into passivity, to ignore your role as leader. This is the temptation to disengage, to walk away. The temptations to become a tyrant or to abdicate will be constant. You must prepare yourself for it."

"So, how will I know when I'm fulfilling my kingly role correctly?"

"When you are engaging to glorify God by providing for your children's material and emotional needs, you are probably on the correct path. I'm sorry that between child support and your own personal expenses, you don't have much left over, but providing materially for your children is a key component of your kingly role. The 'Deadbeat Dad' thing is a horrible abdication of responsibility. What is truly key, however, is that as fathers we should not seek to glorify ourselves. We need to seek to glorify God *through* our service to our families. Living out our kingly roles is establishing God's rules in your home to serve your family, rather than your own rules to serve yourself. Living out your kingly role is meant to be an act of worship that creates an inviting space for our families to join us in worshipping God. Our homes should be emotionally safe and spiritually safe. If our kingly actions either make our homes feel unsafe or drive our families away from worship, we're probably doing something wrong."

Brian blinked slowly as he considered the enormity of what Peter had said. Worse, this was only one of three roles. There were two more roles yet to cover.

Peter continued, "What makes living out our kingly role so difficult in America today is that no one wants to hear it. Men having a kingly role is seen as denigrating women, as if every man is going to immediately use his authority to subjugate everyone living under the same roof with him. Remember when you thought we might need bulletproof vests to discuss these things in a public setting? This topic is incendiary today. People don't want to hear it. Personally, I think their concern is legitimate; the kingly role of men can be easily abused. But the answer is not to strip men of their role; the answer is to train men to fulfill their roles correctly."

"Like what you're doing with me," Brian said.

"Exactly. The temptation you will constantly face will be to corrupt your kingly role. Just remember that when King Jesus came, he did not come to be served, he came to serve.[15] Unfortunately, the temptation you will face is more than in the kingly role; it is in your priestly and prophetic roles too. In your priestly role, you will be tempted in two ways. On the one hand, you will be tempted to ignore your children and your family, to not engage in the hard work of nurturing them. Brian, you have already experienced how hard this is. It's easy to give in to fatigue. The moment you do that, you cease to nurture your children. But the opposite is also true, and this is the second way you will be tempted. You will be tempted to make your children the center of your universe, so that you are always available to them without any boundaries at all. If you ignore your children, they will grow up feeling unloved, but if you are always at their beck and call, they will grow up thinking the world revolves around them."

"Oy," Brian said. "How do I balance *that*?"

Peter laughed. "I don't think anyone really balances it. The temptation you face will be to run to one extreme or the other. The trick to fulfilling your priestly role is to always pray for your children. Seek God's guidance for specifics and trust that God will work with your children over time.

"And finally, the temptation to corrupt your prophetic role, your responsibility to teach your children about God, will come from two different directions. On the one hand, you will be tempted to abdicate your role either to your children's mother or perhaps your church's youth group. On the other hand, you'll be tempted to ram your beliefs down their throats so that they learn to resent God. Your prophetic role requires you to plant seeds with your kiddos. Not every planted seed will grow, but if you can plant enough seeds, trust that God will take care of the growth."[16]

"It seems to me that the temptations of my roles as prophet, priest, and king are the temptations to run to the extremes," Brian said. "Are you going to tell me that the middle road is always the best, to do all things in moderation? That's hardly original advice."

Peter shook his head. "No, that's not what I'm saying. What I'm saying is that we need to be deliberate in how we fulfill our roles. If we allow things to just happen, to just naturally take their course, then we will be tempted to abuse our roles either through ignoring them or going over the top with them. I have yet to give you what the Bible teaches about redeeming children, and the redemption of your children will go a long way to shaping how you will know if you are on the right or wrong track. I find it interesting that for all the talk about fatherhood in Genesis, the father's redemption of the firstborn is not present."

"How come?"

"I'm not sure. My best guess is that a father redeeming his firstborn would not make sense until a major act of God demonstrated what redemption looks like. When God led the children of Israel out of Egypt, with the parting of the Red Sea, taking them to safety, and providing for their needs, people could see what redemption looked like. Only after that could the redemption of the firstborn make sense."

"Okay, so what does the redemption of the firstborn look like?"

Peter smiled his crooked smile. "You're not ready for that yet." He checked his watch. "This is a good place to stop. Let me leave you with this. As you continue to work on the answers to your questions, evaluate how you are currently doing. Remember that because of the Fall, you will be tempted to move between two extremes, by either overdoing each role or disengaging and abdicating it. Both are wrong. So, the first thing to do is to determine which extreme you habitually run to with each role. However, it's not enough to just avoid the extremes. You need to decide *which* middle course you will navigate, and you must know why you made that choice. That's the second thing you need to start doing. Make a deliberate decision of which middle course you will navigate for each role."

"What are the options?" Brian asked.

"Think of it this way. You are the captain of a ship and must navigate your ship between two islands. The islands are a mile apart from each other. If you navigate directly at one of the islands, you will run aground. So, which path will you choose?"

"Um . . . anything in between would work."

"In one sense, yes. But the captain of a ship doesn't have the luxury to just wing it. Ships don't stop quickly, nor do they turn on a dime. He needs to be deliberate in his decisions. He must set a course and keep it. He can change it later as the need arises, but the captain must set a course between the islands. That is what you need to do. You need to set a course. You can change it later, but you must be deliberate and set a course. The options are numerous. Pick what works best for your situation."

"Okay, I'll set a course."

"Good deal. Remember also to keep journaling. And with that, I need to go."

Summary of Key Points

- There is no one-size-fits-all, cookie-cutter approach to fatherhood.

- Adam's position in the Garden was one of trust and friendship.

- "Buddy-buddy" language in prayer is dangerous. We can never lose sight of the fact that we are addressing our king and creator.

- God created us to be fathers so we can understand what His fatherhood over us looks like. We become fathers to our children so they can see the fatherhood of God, and so we can understand how to be better children of God.

- Fencing the law is putting extra precautions around something God said not to do. Fencing the law may have benefits, but we must always remember to never put words in God's mouth.

- A person cannot be tempted with something he does not want. Temptation only works because the person *wants* the temptation.

- Adam and Eve represent two major ways people rebel against God. Those two ways are (a) being foolishly deceived, and (b) being deliberately conniving.

- Men are tempted in their kingly role to either (a) become a tyrant, or (b) to disengage completely.

• Living out the kingly role is meant to be an act of worship that creates an inviting space for our families to join us in worshipping God.

• Men are tempted in their priestly role to either (a) disengage from the hard work of nurturing your family, or (b) make your family the center of your universe instead of God.

• Men are tempted in their prophetic role to either (a) abdicate the responsibility to someone else, or (b) to be so forceful with their teaching that the children grow up resenting their father's beliefs.

• We must be deliberate with our roles. If we allow things to just happen and take their natural course, we will be tempted to either ignore the roles or to go over the top with them.

5 Covering, Banishment, and Redemption

Genesis 3 and 4

The rain was coming down steadily when Brian pulled up. Amazingly, he was on time. They got the kids transferred quickly, hugs were skipped, and they drove off. Brian hustled into the restaurant with little water droplets rolling down the back of his shirt. Combined with the air-conditioning, it was frigid. He shivered.

He found Peter; they got their food and sat down. Brian mimicked Peter globbing ketchup on fries as well as eating them. Then he joined Peter saying, "Mmm-mmm-mmm. Lord, have mercy, a sinner." Peter smiled his crooked smile and half laughed. "You're mocking me, aren't you?"

Brian, channeling his inner Eddie Haskell, assumed a look of pure innocence. "No. I'm just joining you in the opening ritual. I want to be just like my mentor."

Peter laughed. "That's a lot of sarcasm for a young man, but I'll humor you. Okay, so how did it go with the kids?"

"It was okay, I guess. Megan wanted to play Chutes & Ladders again. I didn't. It's a really boring game. But I played, anyway. It was all right, just not as fun as last time. Last time it was new; this time, it was just playing the game. Plus, it was a tough week at work. I was pretty whipped. I also took them back to the park to play, and then we did ice cream. Dinner, nighttime routine, morning routine, church, lunch, and then get ready to leave. I don't know. It was a bit of a nothing weekend."

"Don't be too hard on yourself," Peter replied. "First, the fact that Megan wanted to play Chutes & Ladders again tells me she really enjoyed the previous weekend. Additionally, kids need routine. I'm glad you played the game with them. It helps to establish a routine. You don't have to keep playing the same game; you can introduce others. But having a regular time to just play together is a wonderful routine."

"That's not a bad idea. But with Brian Jr., it's tough to find games he can play."

"That's true. You could get a set of blocks and build something together. It doesn't always have to be a board game. The important part of this routine is that you have a regular and consistent time to play together with your children. Not every one of those times will be a breakthrough moment. But they will become an important way you connect with your kiddos. One day, your playtime will become cherished memories for both you and them. You have the start of something good going; stick with it."

"I will. So, what do you have for me today?"

"Hang on. The last time I asked you to chart your course for each role between the two extremes. Tell me about that. Which extreme do you tend to for each role?"

Brian shifted uncomfortably. "This one was hard because I feel like a fish out of water when it comes to my kids. I feel like I don't know what I'm doing, so it's tough to evaluate which extreme I run to. All I have are guesses."

"That's okay," Peter said soothingly. "Most fathers feel like they don't know what they're doing. Sometimes we just need to start where we're at and go forward from there. As we walk through what the Bible says about fatherhood, you will be forced to consider who God really is and who you really are. This is a journey of God-discovery and self-discovery. That's hard, but there's also some good news here. As you examine yourself in the light of what the Bible says, you will not only become a better father, but you will also get to know God more. And the more you know God, the more you know yourself. There's a lot going on here. Don't be surprised that it's difficult."

Brian nodded. "Okay." He took a breath before continuing. "Well, in my kingly role, I tend toward abdication. I feel like I don't know what I'm doing, and I get frustrated with my children easily. Sometimes I feel like they're not really my kids. It feels like they're Bethany's kids, and I'm just the babysitter. And so, it's easy to grind to a halt. I have to keep reminding myself that they are my kids and force myself to stay engaged. When I get frustrated, I get angry, and I snap at my children. That's not creating an emotionally safe environment. I hate when I snap at them."

"Just keep in mind that this is a normal reaction. A lot of fathers get frustrated with their kids, and they get angry. When men feel incompetent as you do with your kids, they tend to handle it badly. You will gain competency, but it will take some time. Just remember to love your kids and that your kids love you. There is only one perfect father, our heavenly Father. All the rest of us are engaged in various levels of screwing everything up."

"I'm the same with my prophetic role too. I tend to abdicate mainly because I don't know what I'm talking about. I mean, I read the Bible, but it's not like I could teach it, certainly not like you. I'm not that smart. So, my course with both roles will be to avoid running into the island of disengagement, to use your ship and island analogy from last time. For my kingly role, I will focus on creating an emotionally safe space for Megan and Brian Jr. I think that keeps me engaged and provide something they need right now. As for my prophetic role, I want to read a little of the Bible to them as part of our nighttime routine. I can't teach the Bible, but I can read it to them. I bought a paraphrased version of the Bible written for small children. Hopefully, it's age appropriate for them."

"Brian, I love this. This is a great plan. Well done. Now, tell me about your priestly role."

"I think this is the role I over-engage with because I don't know what I'm doing. I know if anything happens to them, I'll never hear the end of it from Bethany. Therefore, I tend to be a helicopter dad who is always protecting them from every danger, both real and perceived in my imagination . . . and I have a *very* active imagination!"

Peter laughed. "So, what's the plan to handle this?"

"Well, part of the helicopter dad tendency is that I don't let the kids do anything or solve any problems. On Saturday, Megan struggled to open a packet of crackers. My first instinct was to reach over and open it for her. Instead, I took a deep breath and then showed her how to open them. She struggled because her finger dexterity is still developing, but she eventually got it. I want to start looking for more opportunities like that to help them grow by solving their own problems, rather than solving their problems for them because it's easier and faster."

Peter nodded in approval. "This is a good plan to start with. It will change and develop over time, but I like what you're choosing to focus on to start. I think your kiddos will be grateful for what you're doing."

Opening his Bible to Genesis 3, Peter placed it on the table between them. "All right, let's get back to the Bible. Last time we looked at the Fall itself. We saw that Eve was deceived, but Adam was not. There was something conniving and calculating about what Adam did. And then we considered how the Fall affected Adam's prophetic, priestly, and kingly roles. Today, I want to start by pulling together two threads of what happened to Adam and Eve. In Genesis 1, we saw what it meant to be created in the image of God. Specifically, we talked about how the original audience would have understood the image of God. Do you remember?"

"Yes. They were images of the king, his representatives. They marked his dominion. And they were sometimes used to test the loyalty of his subjects."

"Good. Remember also that what someone did to the image, they also did to God."

Brian interjected, "Yeah, I remember. If I knelt to the image, it was like kneeling to the king; if I slapped the image, it was like slapping the king. It let the king know about the loyalty of his subjects because they didn't have opinion polls back then."

"Well done, you remember correctly. Now, let's tie that in with the temptation of the serpent. When the serpent came into the Garden, he did so with the specific intent to tempt Adam and Eve. But notice in verse 1, he starts by speaking to the woman. So, Brian, let me ask you this: why did the serpent choose to start with Eve?"

"Because she was the easiest to lure into temptation. She was standing by the tree, and he probably knew that she wanted to be tempted."

Peter waited before responding. "Your answer isn't wrong; it's just incomplete. Think about it some more."

Brian furrowed his brow in thought. He absently took a bite of his chicken finger as he considered his answer. "You're asking why the serpent started with Eve instead of Adam. Well, if he tempted Adam and Adam did not eat the fruit, the woman probably would have been impervious to temptation at that point."

"Good," Peter said, encouraging Brian to continue.

"But let's say Adam succumbed and ate the fruit. The expectation was that the fruit was poisonous and that it would kill them immediately. If Adam ate it and died, Eve would not have. She would only have been guilty of being tempted, not of actually disobeying God."

"Good, you're on the right track. Keep going."

"However, if the serpent got Eve to eat the fruit in Adam's presence—" Suddenly, Brian's eyes got wide. "Then Adam had *already* fallen because he failed to fulfill his kingly, priestly, and prophetic roles! Adam's fall wasn't just eating the fruit; it was failing in the roles he was given by God!"

"You're doing great, but I want to clarify something. Christians have long made the distinction between sins of omission and sins of commission. A sin of omission is failing to do something I ought to do. A sin of commission is doing something I ought not to do. So, up to the point where Eve eats of the fruit before Adam does, who is guilty of what?"

"Eve is guilty of a sin of commission because she ate the fruit God specifically told her not to eat. But Adam is guilty of a sin of omission because he failed to fulfill his duty."

"Very good. Now, what else is Adam guilty of when he eats the fruit?"

"He's guilty of the same sin of commission because he ate the fruit that God told him not to. That means Eve was guilty of the sin of commission, but Adam was guilty both of a sin of omission and the sin of commission."

"Exactly. But like you said, if Adam ate the fruit and Eve decided not to, then the serpent's goal would have only been partly realized. Adam would still have been guilty of the sins of commission and omission. But if Eve did not eat the fruit, she would have been in the clear. That was a result the serpent wanted to avoid. By starting with Eve, so long as Adam did nothing to stop Eve, the serpent tempted both to fall. That Adam subsequently ate the fruit, too, was just icing on the cake for the serpent."

"Does that make Adam more guilty than Eve?" Brian asked.

Peter shrugged. "Well, when you're talking about guilty before the eternal God, I'm not sure 'more guilty' makes a lot of sense. I think what the author is trying to show here is that the sin of Adam and Eve was complete, that they were without excuse. Even though they will both try to make excuses when God confronts them, these are poor attempts to shift the blame off themselves. Remember previously when Eve saw that the fruit was good for food, a delight to the eyes, and desirable to make one wise, we saw that it pointed to her mind, her emotions, and her will. It was the totality of Eve. With Adam, we see that he fell through sins of both omission and commission. Both fell deliberately, and they had no excuse. Eve may have been deceived, but there was still something very deliberate in her choice.”

“Wow, every way this story gets turned, it was a total fail on their part.”

“Yes, it really was a total fail. But now, let's go deeper with this story. I want you to think through how all of this would have sounded to the original audience. Remember that Adam and Eve were created in the image of God. If that's the case, then who was the real target of the temptation? Who was the serpent *really* attacking?”

Brian thought about it before answering tentatively. “God?”

Peter nodded.

“But how can you tempt God to sin?” Brian asked.

“You can't, and the serpent knows it. So, if he isn't trying to tempt God, then what is he trying to do?”

Brian considered the question as he munched on a French fry. Finally, he shrugged, unsure of the answer.

“Remember that for the original audience, the image of the king was a sign of the king's authority. What does it say about a king that he is unable to protect his own images? You see, the *real* target of the serpent was neither Adam nor Eve; it was God. The serpent was attempting to show God as weak, ineffectual, and not very powerful. He's trying to show that God isn't a *real* king because a real king can protect his images. If God was too weak to protect his images—and remember that the images of Adam and Eve were the pinnacle of God's creation—then why should anyone follow him? Just as the serpent had rejected God's authority, he is trying to show that everyone should join him in his rejection of God's authority. And, worse, this isn't the totality of the serpent's scheming. He is trying to put God on the horns of a dilemma. On the one hand, God promised death to Adam and Eve if they ate the fruit. If they died, then God was unable to protect his images from mortal danger. This would mean he was powerless to protect his images. That's the first horn of the dilemma. The second is this; if God failed to execute judgment on Adam and Eve, if he failed to fulfill his word and remove the death penalty, then God was not one who could be trusted to keep his word. It would turn God into a liar. At this point, the serpent thinks he has God in an impossible situation, a dilemma He can't get out of without compromising either His power or His character. Either way, the serpent will be able to say that God is not a *real* king who should be trusted or followed."

"Wow," Brian said. "This is really messed up."

"It is."

"So, how does God get out of the dilemma?"

"Well, before we get to that, I want to pull the thread on this a little more. I want you to see that the serpent was trying to attack God by attacking His images. If what someone does to the image of God is a surrogate for what we do to God, then his images can be targeted in lieu of attacking God directly. In other words, God is a spiritual being. You can't hit God, punch Him, kick Him, or anything like that. However, you *can* hit, punch, and kick His image, a human being. You can't slap God, but you can slap His image. You can't abuse or manipulate God, but you can abuse or manipulate His image. You can't tempt God to sin, but you can tempt His images to sin. Ever since the Fall, we have seen the same thing play out in human history. People want to lash out against God, and they do so by lashing out at other people. I can't hit God, but I can hit His image. I can't abuse God, but I can abuse His image."

"Okay, I think I see what you're saying. But what does this have to do with fatherhood?"

"Quite a bit. Every father was once a child, a child who has a past. The trauma of childhood often gets played out when the traumatized child becomes a parent. The abuse may have been physical, emotional, or sexual. However, that abuse will spill over into his role as a father if it isn't addressed. And what we see here is a way to address it. When a child is abused, how much of the abuse was really targeting God rather than the one who was abused? We can't physically hit God, but we can physically hit His image. We can't emotionally manipulate God, but we can emotionally manipulate His image. And when it comes to sexual abuse, that's not about sex; sexual abuse is about power. It's about exercising power over someone. We can't overpower God, but we can overpower His image. Now, Brian, I'm not implying that you have been either the victim or the perpetrator of child abuse. But as people, we will always suffer abuse at one time or another, and grabbing hold of this truth will help you to process it. When the victim understands that he was not the real target of the abuse, it gives him space to process it and even to forgive without making any excuses for the abuser. It gives space for the victim to heal without allowing the abuser to wriggle out of taking responsibility for what he has done. Well, his or her responsibility; women can be abusers too. For the victim, it helps him—or her—to see his real issue is that he was abused as a surrogate for someone trying to attack God.

"Brian, if you haven't been the victim of abuse to this point, that's fantastic. But I bring this up now because one day you will be sitting in my seat talking to a young father, showing him all that I am showing to you. And if you discover he was the victim of abuse, you will need to know what to say. Show him this passage and explain it to him. Give him the opportunity to get some mental space between himself and his abuser. Folks who have suffered abuse tend to deal with all sorts of baggage about their worth as a person, with feelings of worthlessness, isolation, anger, abandonment, dand feeling unlovable. When those feelings spill over into his own parenting, it's awful for the children. But when the victim can see that the abuse was targeting God, it changes the dynamic of it. It doesn't excuse it any more than it excused the serpent, but it can create space for healing to occur."

"What about parents who were not abusive so much as unloving or even . . .." Brian's voice trailed off.

"Did not want their children?" Peter asked. Brian nodded, not wanting to speak for fear his voice would crack. "Some parents are unable to show love while others bail out on their children because the parent feels worthless. But whatever the reason, when a parent fails to love his own child or fails to love them to the point that he abandons his own flesh and blood, you can be sure that there are some serious issues going on there. Is he fighting God? Probably. Every case is unique. If he leaves because he suffers from substance abuse, I don't know that he is in his right mind. Given how addictive that stuff can be, I'd hesitate to call it fighting God or even running away from God in that case. Yet, although addiction is understandable, it is no excuse for abandoning a child."

Brian realized Peter was looking right through him. Did he know Brian's dad left his family when he was young? Brian didn't want to know. It was time to change the subject. "Do you really think one day I'll be explaining all this to someone else?"

"Yes, absolutely," Peter answered with finality, as if the answer was painfully obvious. "When you finally get your head around all this and start living it out, it will be like you can't wait to tell someone about it."

"Even to the point of accosting a stranger in the parking lot of a restaurant?" Brian asked, remembering how he first met Peter.

Peter laughed. "Well, let's just say that I recognized your situation clearly and was ready to help."

"That, and you wanted some French fries."

"Exactly." They both laughed. "Okay, let's get back to your earlier question: How did God resolve the dilemma? The short answer is that He resolved it with grace and the promise of a redeemer. I want to make sure you understand this because it has a direct bearing on fatherhood. Let's look at God's response to the Fall. In Genesis 3:14, He curses the serpent. But in the next verse, He provides a promise."

> And I will put enmity
> Between you and the woman,
> And between your seed and her seed;
> He shall bruise you on the head,
> And you shall bruise him on the heel. (Genesis 3:15)

"We've already talked about this verse," Brian said. "You said that God showed grace by delaying death, that there would be good times intermixed with the bad times before a person dies. And you also said that it was the promise of Jesus."

"That's right. Now let's look at it more closely. The promise of Jesus is the promise of a redeemer, one who will come to redeem Adam and Eve and their children from the curse of sin, or the penalty for disobeying God. It is the promise to redeem them back to the state God created them to be. So, the question for Adam and Eve is this: What will that redeemer look like? Look at 3:21. *And the LORD God made garments of skin for Adam and his wife and clothed them.'*

"Prior to this, Adam and Eve did not wear clothing. This is a picture of innocence, but the intent was not for them to always be naked. There is a built-in expectation that they would be clothed eventually. The question is, clothed in what? For the original audience, clothing was a picture of righteousness. Prior to the Fall, Adam and Eve had not sinned, so they had nothing to hide. Had they resisted the temptation of the serpent and not eaten the forbidden fruit, they would have been clothed in righteousness. However, they did eat the forbidden fruit, and now their nakedness reflects their shame. What was the first thing Adam and Eve did after eating the fruit? Look at verse 7."

> Then the eyes of both of them were opened, and they knew
> that they were naked; and they sewed fig leaves together and
> made themselves loin coverings. (Genesis 3:7)

"They sewed together fig leaves. In an instant, their nakedness went from innocence to shame, and the first thing they attempted to do was to cover their shame with fig leaves. As we read it, there is something pathetic about their feeble attempts to cover themselves. Instead of being clothed in righteousness by God, they are clothing themselves with leaves. Now in verse 21, God makes clothing from the skin of animals. As the reader, we should ask why does he do that? What's wrong with clothing made from plants?" Peter tugged the collar of his shirt. "My shirt is made from a blend of cotton and other plant-based material. Much of the best clothing is made from plants or from shearing an animal's coat. Animal skins were previously used for cold weather, but not for the clothing we wear all the time. The original audience would have read this knowing that the animal skins were not for everyday wear. This is something special. God does it as a demonstration, as an object lesson to teach Adam and Eve.

"What is God teaching? He is teaching them three things. First, He is teaching them that they need grace. Adam and Eve's feeble attempt to cover their shame is not enough. They need God to graciously cover their shame. They are unable to do it on their own, and the grace that is needed requires the shedding of blood. Their sin is serious; it requires blood to be shed. But rather than using their own blood immediately, the blood of another will act as a substitute. Second, God is teaching them grace by sacrificing blood for them. God does not require Adam and Eve to provide a sacrifice for themselves so their shame can be covered; he provides the sacrifice himself. And third, notice that God clothes them. The word *clothed* in the original Hebrew means literally to dress them, like a servant would dress his master. God does not show them a half-hearted, reluctant grace, or even a begrudging grace. He shows them grace within the context of a servant. God is demonstrating his love for them in that although they have sinned, he is providing for them and serving them tenderly. He has not reversed the reality that Adam and Eve will experience physical death;

he has simply delayed it so they can know the extent of God's love for them and the extent of His grace toward them. What we see here is a picture of God's love for Adam and Eve like a father's love for his children even when they fail. He will punish them as he said he would, but he still loves them. He hates having to punish them, so he mixes his punishment with grace."

Brian let out a low whistle. "I've never seen any of this before. To be honest, I used to think God was being a bit stingy giving them rough animal skins instead of decent clothing before he kicked them out of the Garden. But this is totally different."

"It is, and it gets to be more. You see, the three things God is showing them have double meanings. Remember that verse 15 was the promise of a redeemer, the one who will crush the head of the serpent and set things right?"

"Yeah. That's Jesus."

"Right. In sacrificing an animal and clothing Adam and Eve, God is showing them what the redeemer will be like when he comes. First, their sin requires the shedding of blood so that their sins can be adequately covered. That is the first hint that when the redeemer comes, he will redeem by causing God to shed blood. As it turns out, it will be the shedding of Jesus's blood on the cross. Second, just as God provided the animals that were sacrificed for Adam and Eve, he will also provide the redeemer who will be sacrificed. And third, just as God clothed Adam and Eve as a servant, so the redeemer will come as a servant. Jesus said he came not to be served, but to serve and to give his life as a ransom for many."[17]

"He's showing them all that just by clothing them?"

"Yes. And let me show you that they understood it. Take a look at Genesis 4:1. This is where Eve gives birth to her first child.

Now the man had relations with his wife Eve, and she conceived and gave birth to Cain, and she said, "I have gotten a manchild with the help of the LORD."

Peter pointed to the verse. "Eve names her child Cain. The name is a play on the Hebrew word for *gotten* or *begotten*. But notice that she says she did it with the help of the Lord. This is a statement of renewed faith. She is saying that she did not do this on her own; the Lord was involved. Additionally, she is stating this in expectation that the progeny of one child of hers will be the promised redeemer. From her point of view, maybe it's Cain, maybe it's another child she will give birth to, or perhaps it will be a descendant yet to be born. Regardless, Eve is stating her trust in the goodness of the Lord to deliver on his promise of a redeemer. In this one terse statement, the author lets the reader know that Eve understood what God said and did when He clothed them in animal skins and He promised a redeemer. The skin wasn't meant for everyday clothing; it was special clothing to make a statement. And Eve understood the statement."

"Did Adam understand it too?" asked Brian.

Peter nodded. "Eventually, yes, but that involves another story. I want to stay on this topic of the redeemer because it is important for fatherhood. The importance is not immediately obvious. I need to connect a few dots for you to get there."

"I'm ready," Brian said. "Go for it."

"The issue involves how a child bonds to his parents. The bond between a mother and her child is accomplished initially through biological processes. As the child grows in the womb, the mother's voice can be heard by the child, and the child is born with the ability to recognize the voice of his mother. After birth, the child continues to bond with his mother as the mother holds him and feeds him. The child is born completely dependent on his mother to care for his physical needs, and she does just that. Because of this, the initial bonding between a mother and child is driven by biological processes, through the constant touching and care for physical needs. The more the mother does her duty, the more opportunities there are for the two to bond. There is a reason why children almost always remember their mothers more fondly than their fathers: the bonding with mothers is driven by biological processes.

"The bonding of a father to his child is different. There are no biological processes that underpin fatherhood. There is no physical need early on that fathers can fulfill better than the child's mother. For the first several years, the father has no significant biological role to play."

"Wait a minute," Brian objected. "Are you saying that fathers are irrelevant to their children?"

"No, not at all. I'm saying that for the first couple of years, fathers do not have a major *biological* role to play. They have an important emotional role to play and they are instrumental in the child reaching maturity but, initially, there is no biological responsibility. Therefore, the bonding between a father and child is different than between a mother and child. It is precisely *because* a father's bonding with his children has no biological underpinning that fathers are so important.

"Try and see things from the perspective of a newborn. This child has spent nine months listening to the voice of his mother. Once born, he is completely dependent on his mother for his physical needs. The person with the same voice that he has grown accustomed to now holds him and feeds him and takes care of him. It is hard for him to know where he stops and the mother begins. There is the constant danger of the child becoming enmeshed with his mother. In fact, the children who have no father figure experience more separation anxiety when first attending school than those who have a father in the home. Why? Because Father is not Mother. He is somebody else, a different person, a different voice. He is always there, perhaps not as much as Mother, but present on a regular basis. The father begins to hold the child, to talk to him, and to play with him. He interacts with the child. When he does those things, the father helps his child to distinguish between his mother and himself. It helps him to understand where he ends and his mother begins. This is a huge step in his development.

"Additionally, mothers and fathers interact with their children differently. Mothers always interact with their children the same way, establishing patterns that the child can count on. A mother establishes structure and routine with the child. Additionally, she tends to interact with the child using a soothing, calming voice. On the other hand, Dad's interaction with his child is normally the polar opposite. Where Mom always approaches the child in the same way, Dad comes at the child from unique angles. He rarely does the same thing twice. Where Mom speaks in soothing tones, Dad speaks in different tones, generally playful ones. Where Mom holds the child, Dad lets the child crawl all over him. Where Mom is the constant in the child's life, the one who is well-known, Dad is the novelty, the one who needs to be explored. Through all of this, Dad becomes the 'other' in the life of a small child, the one who does things differently than Mom does them. This difference is what helps the child separate from Mother in a healthy way so that the two are no longer enmeshed. When there is an *other* in the life of the child who is completely separate from Mother, the child begins to distinguish between self and Mother."

"Let me ask you a question. Bethany has always corrected me on how I interact with our children. It seemed like I could never do anything right. Are you telling me I don't have to listen to her anymore?"

"No, you should always listen. If what she's talking about involves the safety of your children, you need to listen to her carefully. And, as a rule of thumb, you should always listen; you just don't have to comply. Mothers can get very protective of their children, especially when someone is doing something differently than the way the child is used to. But sometimes different is a good thing; it helps the child.

There is something beneficial to just interacting with your child in the manner that is natural for you. Only don't overdo it. Too much change all at once is not good. If the different way of doing something is too much for the child, the child will let you know almost immediately. If they start crying, you've gone too far. In your case, Brian, you've already begun implementing changes with "Mom's house, Mom's rules; Dad's house, Dad's rules." It's OK to do things a little differently; children need some of that from their fathers.

"Now, the reason I'm belaboring the point that Father is 'other' or 'another' as separate and different from Mother is not just for their emotional development as a young child. As kids get a little older, they need this 'other' for another reason too. They need to know that they are loved by someone other than their mother. Remember, the bonding between a mother and child is driven by strong biological processes. However, as the child grows less dependent on Mother for his physical needs, he needs to know there is another who loves and accepts him. A child's sense of worth is based in large part on the love and acceptance of his father, that 'other' in his life. A child can feel secure in his mother's love, but if he does not feel equally secure in his father's love, in the love of that 'other' person, then the child will struggle with feeling unloved and unwanted. He will struggle with feelings of worthlessness."

Brian shifted in his seat.

Peter continued. "What a child needs most from his father is to be redeemed. He needs to be told time and time again how much the father loves him and is proud to be the child's father. The child needs to rest as comfortably in the love of his father as he does in the love of his mother. This is not achieved through biological processes. Well, not primarily. Don't underestimate the value of a good hug. Children need appropriate physical contact with their fathers. But the primary ways a child experiences love from his father are through the father's words and actions, through what he says and what he does. It's not enough to say it and not do it, nor is it enough to do it and not say it. Children need both. You may never know how much it means to a child when his father hugs him and says, 'I love you, and I'm proud of you.' Or maybe, 'I love you, and I'm always rooting for you.' If your actions match your words, it can truly transform the lives of your children."

"You say that words and actions have to match. But how can actions match the words of 'I love you, and I'm proud of you'?"

"That's a great question, Brian. I'm glad you asked it. However, I've already given you the answer. Do you remember?"

Brian searched his mind, trying to replay the conversation with Peter. After a moment, he gave up. "No, I don't."

"Do you remember when we talked about the three roles of fatherhood?"

"Yeah, the prophetic role, the priestly role, and the kingly role. So what?"

"Living those out is the way you make your actions match your words. Again, think about it from a child's perspective. A child probably doesn't recognize when his material needs are provided for, but you can sure bet he'll know when they're not being met. However, the kingly role is also about providing an emotionally safe place to live. That's the father's kingly role lived out in a way the child understands. Additionally, the priestly role is caring for the child. Children know when you care for them. Finally, the prophetic role is a teaching one. Children know when you are preparing them for life. When a father lives out his roles, the child understands his father's love. When he backs up those actions with words of love and affirmation, the child will rest secure in his father's love.

"This leads to my assignment for you this week. I want you to start thinking about ways you can redeem your children. Redeeming your children is not less than words, but it must be more than words. Think about ways you can make your words match your actions. How can you let your kids know you love them, are proud of them, and you're always rooting for them? How can you let them know that they belong to you just as you belong to them? Sometimes you just need to say it directly. Sometimes you need to say it indirectly. So, start thinking about how you can redeem your children so that they know how much you love them."

"Hmm," Brian said with a furrowed brow. "I'll need time to think about that one."

"I totally understand. But I want to give you one more insight into the importance of redeeming your children. Redeeming your children is not really about you."

"Wait, it's not?"

"No," Peter replied. "It's about Christ. Remember in the Garden that God clothed Adam and Eve in animal skins as a way of foreshadowing the redeemer who was to come. In the same way, fathers who redeem their children are preparing their children to be redeemed by Christ. Just as the father is 'other' or 'another,' so Christ is truly the 'other' that people seek. However, since Christ is not known in a physical form, it is often difficult for people to understand God's love for us. He does not whisper to us, nor does He give us a physical hug."

"Are you saying that God uses me to whisper to my children and to give them the hugs He cannot give them?"

"Partly, yes. But it's more than that. When a child understands the love and acceptance of his earthly father, it is a bridge to experiencing the love and acceptance of his heavenly father. The father is this 'other' who redeems the child and prepares him to experience the true redemption that is found in Christ. Think of it as training wheels. A child needs training wheels to learn to ride a bike. Eventually, the training wheels come off and the child is free to enjoy riding the bicycle. In the same manner, our earthly fathers are training wheels. They help the child to learn the love and redemption of God in Christ. Eventually, the training wheels come off and the child is free to experience the love and acceptance of God for himself."

"You're making it sound like fathers are disposable."

Peter laughed. "Yeah, you're right. I probably overstated it. But fathers are the most natural bridge to God that a child has. The father is a picture of Christ, the redeemer, who loves and sacrifices and provides and teaches and cares for the child."

"Can't mothers do this?"

"Yes, but not as effectively. Remember, mothers have the privilege of bonding with their children in a very special way that is undergirded by strong biological processes. Don't ever underestimate how important that is to children. However, the very fact that a father's bonding is not supported by biological processes is what makes him the ideal parent to serve as a bridge to God. God is a nonphysical being. Our relationship with Him has no biological support structures, just like a child's relationship with his father. So, it is the father who acts as the primary conduit of a child's spiritual formation. Yes, there are exceptions, but they are just that—exceptions. The rule is that fathers have the most influence on a child's spiritual development. I believe this is why when fathers don't go to church or when children grow up without a father, they often walk away from church as adults. It's not the only reason, but it's a big one. And that's why I'm proud of you for taking your children to church. When you do that, you're continuing to act as a bridge between your children and God. Redeeming your children is not just a matter of redeeming them to yourself; it's a matter of redeeming them to the Lord."

Brian exhaled. "That's deep."

"It is. But I never said any of this was going to be easy, did I?"

Brian shook his head.

"Okay, so here's what I want you to do. When you're planning your week, I want you to ask how you will redeem your children this week. It doesn't have to be anything major. Small consistencies are much better than a few over-the-top things. But plan it into your schedule as you are able. How will you redeem your children this week? And then at your end-of-week review, ask how you did redeem your children this week. Can you do that?"

"Sure."

"Good." Peter looked at his watch with a start. "Wow, this has been a long one. I need to get going. See you next time?"

"Absolutely!"

Summary of Key Points

• The trauma of a man's childhood gets played out when he becomes a parent. His trauma will spill over to his family if it is not addressed.

• Abusing God's image is really an attempt to abuse God. You cannot hit God because He is a spiritual being, but you can hit His image. This gives space for the abused to heal without making excuses for the abuser. It also forces the abuser to face the real issues behind his actions.

• When Adam and Eve fell, their nakedness was turned from innocence to shame.

• The bonding of a mother and child is supported through natural, biological processes. The bonding of father and child has no equivalent. Therefore, fatherhood does not happen naturally; it must be deliberately supported.

• The "otherness" of fathers makes them the ideal bridge to understanding God.

• Children need to be "redeemed" by their fathers, for the father to declare that he is the child's father. This redemption points to the redemption of God in Christ.

Epilogue: What About Moms?

As pointed out in the introduction, next to nothing has been said to this point about the role of mothers in a child's development. The focus of Genesis 2–3 is on Adam, not Eve, so we should not be surprised that there is little discussion of motherhood. Although motherhood was baked into the original design of God's creation (Genesis 1:28, 3:16), the text does not have any reference to it until Genesis 4, which is where the next book in this series will begin.

However, it seems to me that a few words should be said on the issue of motherhood. Chapter 2 reflects my opinion that the entire discussion of the relationship between males and females has become incendiary. Any deviation from the cultural orthodoxy results in flaming, scorn, derision, and canceling, all of which is the twenty-first-century equivalent of being burned in effigy. To make matters worse, there is an overly simplistic approach to what passes for a discussion on cultural matters. Either someone entirely supports position A or they are really supporting position Z. And, naturally, position Z is totally outrageous and unacceptable. For example, "Either you support (insert your preferred political party here), or you support throwing people in gulags." "Either you support teachers' unions, or you don't want disadvantaged children educated." "Either you support school vouchers, or you don't want to see disadvantaged children educated." If you want more examples, they are easy to find. Just browse your social media feed!

The unspoken assumption with this approach is that there is nothing in between A and Z, nor is there a third option. For folks who engage in this kind of thinking, I respectfully suggest that the relationship between males and females is too complex for such a reductive view. When it comes to the relationship of men and women, fathers and mothers, there is a lot of nuance in the biblical teaching that defies any attempt to boil it down to a social media meme; it is too complex.

If I were forced to reduce biblical teaching on this subject into a meme, it would be this: the Bible teaches egalitarianism between men and women in the workplace and politics, but complementarianism in the home and church. In the workplace and in politics, if an individual woman can do the job and is willing to do it (and in the case of politics she can be elected), have at it! Although there will be a few set-asides in which women will generally be unable to do the job equally to men, those jobs are normally professional athletes. Even in construction, there is enough machinery designed to preserve people's backs that the size and strength differences between men and women are an unnecessary concern. Whether women actually *want* those jobs is another matter; there is no biblical concern with egalitarianism in the workplace and in politics.

The home and church, however, are a different matter. As discussed in chapter 5, the otherness of the father is critical for both the emotional and spiritual development of a child. The father helps the child to avoid enmeshing with the mother, to bond with another person and, ultimately, to establish his or her own identity as a person. Although many have attempted to argue that any third person can accomplish this, the research says otherwise, at least regarding the emotional development of the child. Additionally, the "otherness" of the child's father is a bridge to the child's heavenly father. The child's biological father is the absolute best person to guide the child's emotional and spiritual development unless, of course, the father is a clear danger to the child. Mothers have the benefit of physical processes that bond mother and child closely so that the child knows unconditional love; fathers have the benefit of providing the foundation of a life of confidence, emotional stability, and spiritual depth. Each has their role to play, and both roles are equally important. However, no matter how complementary the roles are, they cannot be performed by the same person. Thus, fathers and mothers, men and women, have complementary but different roles within the home.

Further, the Bible teaches male headship of the home. This is not endorsing male dominance. It is simply the recognition that there will be times when disagreements cannot be resolved through compromise. When that happens, someone has to make the final decision, and that person is the husband. This is something we understand instinctively in the workplace. Someone in the organization must be responsible to make a final decision, someone with whom the buck stops, to paraphrase Harry Truman. No one complains that this position is unfair; the organization will fall apart without it. Yet for some reason, the same need for a final decision-maker in the home is automatically viewed as abusive and unfair. It is considered abusive because people assume it silences the woman and makes her needs, wants, and input valueless, and it is considered unfair because perhaps the woman is the better decision-maker.

Again, it is important to return to the "otherness" of the father. The otherness of the father is to be a bridge to our heavenly father, and as Ephesians 5:25 states, husbands are to love their wives as Christ, also, loves the church. The Bible calls on us to strive for this ideal in our homes even though we will typically fall far short of it. But what happens when the wife begins making all the decisions in the home? The weakness of the unassertive biological father is superimposed on our heavenly father. When Mother bosses Father around, the weakness of the biological father is superimposed on our heavenly father. Mothers must decide what is more important: running their homes in the name of fairness or allowing their husbands to fulfill their role for the sake of her children.

What is true of the home is true in the church. Male leadership of the church is the primary way for people to understand and experience the fatherhood of God. In the New Testament, the focus of fatherhood shifts from biological fatherhood to spiritual fatherhood (e.g., 1 Timothy 1:2,18), a reality that is reflected in the male headship of church leadership.

Moreover, Paul recognizes that as the church spreads across the globe, it will encounter people who have no concept of what a healthy home should look like. Where, then, should these men be trained to lead their homes as Christ leads the church? The answer is in the church itself (1 Timothy 2:11–15; 2 Timothy 2:2). In fact, the qualification for church leadership is that men manage their households well (1 Timothy 3:4–5, 12). For men who grew up without a positive male role model, the church is where they must be trained to become godly men and positive role models for their children. Since fatherhood lacks the biological underpinnings that motherhood has, there is nothing "natural" about it. Fatherhood is a learned position, and the church is where untrained men may learn those skills. Therefore, in the church, women are generally restrained from exercising the kingly, priestly, and prophetic roles over men (1 Timothy 2:11–15) for training purposes. It is not a reflection of a woman's ability in these areas; it reflects the need to train men so that they can lead as God would have them lead in the home.

For many who are committed to full egalitarianism, they will say that this is not fair. In response, I would say that if this were something made up by humans, as many who support full egalitarianism do, then the objection would carry merit. The problem is that this standard does not come from humans; this is from God. All human actions will one day be judged by God, and He is *very* concerned that we treat people justly, according to the guidelines that He has given to us. However, when God sets the boundaries of human behavior, we must understand that there is no set of circumstances in which we will sit in judgment of

God. God will never be judged by humans. People can shake their fists at God all they want—so what? When God sets boundaries, human concepts of "fairness" are neither here nor there. His boundaries are not opinions or a point of view; they are reality. And they are the reality we must deal with. This is His world and His creation. Ultimately, this is His show, not ours. He gets to run it as He sees fit. And if God chose full complementarianism, full egalitarianism, or something in between, there is no rational basis for humans to cry "Foul!" or "Unfair!" When God says this is the way it is, then that is the way it is. Either we accept and obey, or we reject and rebel.[18]

Finally, James 3:1 admonishes men not to seek to become teachers in the church because teachers will incur a stricter judgment. However, because men have a prophetic (read, teaching) role in the home, we men likely will be judged more strictly regarding how and what we taught our children about God. For those who decry male headship is unfair, I ask in return, is it fair that men will face a stricter judgment?

I will leave it to future books in this series to highlight the role of mothers in Scripture and the male–female relationship. This series is focused on fatherhood, but it's not possible to discuss fatherhood completely apart from motherhood. Mothers and fathers are supposed to work as a team, so this series would be both deficient and incomplete if it talked about only half the team. The role of mothers will not be denied, even as this series focuses on fathers.

Be forewarned: the examples of fatherhood in Genesis are often complete trainwrecks. They are examples of the way things should not be rather than positive examples of what should be. Additionally, most of the examples of fatherhood are similarly poor examples of men who fail at fatherhood. There is plenty to learn from negative examples. And there are examples of some who fail at fatherhood and yet see their fatherhood redeemed (notably Adam, Jacob/Israel, and perhaps even Cain, the one who slew his own brother). The Bible's portrayal of fatherhood is not one-sided, in which the men of God are great fathers and unbelievers are terrible fathers. Quite the opposite. There are numerous examples where men of God are very poor fathers while the ungodly are very good fathers. Such portrayals are a complete reversal of our expectations, and they are challenging to work through. But the best teaching comes from the upending of our preconceived notions.

May our God in heaven, his son our Savior, and the Holy Spirit richly bless you and guide you as you work through biblical fatherhood, and in your own fatherhood, whether you are a physical father or a spiritual father . . . or both!

Endnotes

[1] At that time. Since then, more books have been published, but most have fallen into the error of proof-texting the author's view of fatherhood more than systematically drawing out what the Bible taught about it.

[2] Proverbs 16:10; 1 Samuel 12:25

[3] 2 Samuel 12:13

[4] Jeremiah 23:5

[5] Ephesians 6:4; Colossians 3:21

[6] Ephesians 5:25

[7] 1 Timothy 5:8

[8] Deuteronomy 18:21–22.

[9] Exodus 20:7; Deuteronomy 5:11

[10] Ephesians 5:18

[11] Hebrews 12:11 (see Hebrews 12:5–11 for the entire context); Ephesians 6:4; Colossians 2:5; 1 Timothy 4:7–8.

[12] Genesis 3:8

[13] Romans 5:12

[14] Romans 5:12–14

[15] Matthew 20:8; Mark 10:45

[16] 1 Corinthians 3:6.

[17] Matthew 20:28; Mark 10:45.

[18] I know that this is an example of "Either A or Z, nothing in between and no third option" thinking that I rejected earlier. It is not *always* wrong to think this way. Only, one needs to be sure it is correct before tossing it out there. In this case, it works given the nature of the

subject. For social and political issues, it rarely works because there are almost always nuances and exceptions.

About the Author

Tony is the author of *In the Beginning . . . Dads* the first of a planned six-volume series called Fatherhood in Genesis.

As a father, Tony has been a resident father, a nonresident father, and a stepfather. His creative, think outside-the-box approach to fatherhood was the result of a serious study of what the Bible teaches about fatherhood. He learned that God calls all men to fatherhood, whether it is to be a father of his physical children, or to be a spiritual father to other boys. Fatherhood is what defines us as men. It is not just the ability to produce physical children but imparting ourselves as fathers to others that they may see our true Father in heaven.

Tony has a Master's degree from Reformed Theological Seminary, Washington DC and is currently pursuing a Ph.D. in Biblical Studies at Lancaster Bible College. His goal is to teach biblical fatherhood to men, and to equip men to live that calling out and to encourage them to understand their fatherhood in the light of God's Fatherhood of us all.

Tony lives in Southern Maryland with his dog and cat. His children—three of his own and a stepson—are adults and living on their own. He lost his wife to cancer in 2019.

Read more at tonypapadakis.com.

www.ingramcontent.com/pod-product-compliance
Lightning Source LLC
Chambersburg PA
CBHW071327140726
47996CB00005B/1855